All Is Not Loss

All Is Not Loss

The Spirituality of Grief

Duncan MacLaren

CANTERBURY
PRESS

© Duncan MacLaren 2025

First published in 2025 by the Canterbury Press Norwich

Editorial office
3rd Floor, Invicta House
110 Golden Lane,
London EC1Y 0TG, UK
www.canterburypress.co.uk

Canterbury Press is an imprint of Hymns Ancient & Modern Ltd
(a registered charity)

Hymns Ancient & Modern® is a registered trademark of
Hymns Ancient & Modern Ltd
13A Hellesdon Park Road, Norwich,
Norfolk NR6 5DR, UK

All rights reserved. No part of this publication may be reproduced,
stored in a retrieval system, or transmitted,
in any form or by any means, electronic, mechanical,
photocopying or otherwise, without the prior permission of
the publisher, Canterbury Press.

Duncan MacLaren has asserted his right under the Copyright, Designs and
Patents Act 1988 to be identified as the Author of this Work

British Library Cataloguing in Publication data

A catalogue record for this book is available
from the British Library

ISBN: 978 1 78622 613 6

EU GPSR Authorised Representative
LOGOS EUROPE, 9 rue Nicolas Poussin, 17000, LA ROCHELLE, France
E-mail: Contact@logoseurope.eu

No part of this book may be used or reproduced in any manner for the
purpose of training artificial intelligence technologies or systems.

Typeset by Regent Typesetting

Contents

Foreword ix

Acknowledgements xi

Introduction: The Spirituality of Grief xiii

1 Bereavement 1

2 Mortality 19

3 Dependence 34

4 Parting 53

5 Nostalgia 65

6 Failure 81

7 Shame 97

8 Regret 113

9 Forgetting 127

Acknowledgement of Sources 145
Index of Names and Subjects 146

In memory of
Ed Robson
fellow pilgrim
1966–2025

Foreword

by Ian Bradley

Amid so much that seems to be getting worse in our culture and society, one positive and welcome trend is the ending of the taboo that has so long surrounded death and dying. After around 120 years of being swept under the carpet and confined to the closet, death is at last being much more openly acknowledged, talked about and confronted.

This book makes a significant contribution to this welcome and healthy process of opening up conversations about death and bereavement. Its subject is grief – not just the grief that arises from dying and death, but the grief that comes from other forms of loss, including partings, ageing, failures, regrets, guilt and, indeed, the closing of churches – especially pertinent in Scotland just now. With his background as a healthcare chaplain and hospice counsellor, Duncan MacLaren has seen too much to offer easy slogans and shallow comforts. He acknowledges the reality of pain and suffering and the fact that they will never completely go away. Yet he has also experienced enough to come to the realization that, in his words, 'grief may visit us with unexpected gifts', and that it may in time lead to new insights, to deeper contemplation, and to a broader 'universalizing faith'.

As well as being a valuable contribution to the current opening up of taboos around death and dying, *All Is Not Loss* also has much of interest to say on another hot contemporary topic, that of spirituality. We are often told that we are living through a 'spiritual revolution' in which traditional religion is dying and being replaced by a new and more amorphous spirituality.

Duncan MacLaren avoids the negativity about religion that so often surrounds this analysis. He points out the rich resources that religious traditions and institutions have which can help those grieving and consumed with guilt. But his focus is on spirituality, which, he says, has relatively recently come to be associated with the individual rather than the collective. He argues passionately and convincingly here for a more corporate and less individualistic emphasis, defining spirituality as 'connection, insight and growth'. This is a fresh and inspiring read.

Ian Bradley, Emeritus Professor of Cultural and Spiritual History, University of St Andrews

Acknowledgements

Many people have contributed to this book.

The team at Canterbury Press have been unfailingly helpful and professional. I approached them after reading another of their beautifully produced books, and I am grateful for their belief in the project.

Cathy Backett, who has supervised my work for over 20 years, has been a wise and caring companion on my own road of loss and grief. It was one of her pithy insights that first sowed the seed.

Richard Holloway has been a stimulating conversation partner in recent years, and I am grateful to him for reading the manuscript and enlarging my thinking.

Ian Bradley has once again been generous with his time, sharing ideas, reading the text and contributing the Foreword. In writing this book I have often followed his footprints.

Jane MacLaren has listened patiently to various drafts being read aloud and has kept me grounded in the realities that many readers face. Her love and encouragement have been a constant gift.

It has been an immense privilege to accompany grieving people over the years – those who are hurting and bewildered, those living with an incurable illness, their carers, the dying and the bereaved. They have been my teachers.

Ed Robson was a wonderful friend with whom I walked on pilgrimage to the Isle of Iona every year. He was diagnosed with cancer around the time I began writing this book; he died just as I was finishing it. His illness and death surprised and humbled me. I thought I had begun to understand grief; he reminded me that grief is wilder and more mysterious than I had often imagined. This book is dedicated to him.

Duncan MacLaren
July 2025

Introduction:
The Spirituality of Grief

Grief.
It paces the corridors of a childhood home.
It ponders a redundancy notice.
It hides a lover's photo in a breast pocket.
It returns again and again to a fork in the road.
Grief watches from the school gate.
It puzzles over a diagnosis.
It studies the wrinkled face in the mirror.
It straightens empty slippers, or carries a suicide note in a purse.
It weeps for each silent extinction.
Grief pauses at the for-sale sign on an empty church and remembers.

Mostly, we don't see this. People get on with their lives – or not – carrying their griefs deep within. From time to time, feelings surface. Grieving people can be overwhelmed by painful reminders which sweep over them like a powerful wave. These triggers come unexpectedly: a song on a radio; a changing season; a photograph. A young woman told me she had to abandon her basket in the supermarket aisle: she had picked up her husband's favourite cereal before she remembered he was dead.

If grief is everywhere, catching people unawares, where are all these grieving people? Why are the supermarket aisles not filled with them? Once we ask this question, our perceptions may alter. Like the conjurer's sleight of hand, grief can be hidden in plain sight: the girl on the train; the driver in the rear-view mirror; the walker on the beach. Look closer: grief is there.

Pervasive loss

The truth is that grieving people are everywhere. They are not the exception but the norm. They include virtually all of us. Perhaps we are not crying in a parked car or at a lonely café table (although many are). But most of us are carrying the pain of loss just beneath the surface. We wander through the day with blurry, teary eyes; or we feel the ache in our chests and throats from trying to keep our emotions under wraps. Or it may press down upon us: a low-level chronic sadness. Perhaps the loss goes back decades. It hardly bothers us but lurks deep down, like a shipwreck. We don't go there; we've learned to glide over it. There may be no tears, but such battle-hardened losses may be evident in other ways: a brittle, breezy act that covers our fear of what might surface.

If we were to ask people around us why they are sad, perhaps we'd be surprised. It's easy to assume that the lion's share of grief in this life is a consequence of losing loved ones. Yet I am struck by how often the people who come to talk about a bereavement end up focusing on a series of ancillary losses that are connected but different.

Bereavement is only the tip of the iceberg of loss. In the context of therapy, almost everything a client might bring could be traced back to loss of some form or other. This raises the curious possibility that, far from being a rare interruption in our settled lives, loss is woven into the fabric of life. It is present not only in big life events, such as divorce, diagnosis or death, but everywhere. Loss is *pervasive*; we spend our whole lives dealing with it. It follows from this that grief – our natural response to loss – is not a singular reaction to a rare event. It is written into our life stories. *Grief is part of the warp and weft of what it means to be human.*

INTRODUCTION: THE SPIRITUALITY OF GRIEF

The shape of this book

In this book, I am going to look below the waterline at some of the ways in which loss is manifested. What I hope to do in these pages is to stimulate curiosity about the many faces of loss, and what these mean for us. This is not a reference book: my hope is that it will start conversations rather than end them. I don't have 'all the answers', but my hunch is that there is more to loss than meets the eye. Something so universal leaves me wondering if it might harbour more than sheer pain. Put differently, could there be an invitation in loss and grief to spiritual transformation?

Each chapter will focus on a different theme. In Chapter 1, I take up the theme of *bereavement*: the loss of a loved one through death. I explore this complex and familiar grief, charting some of the ways we may recover and grow through grief. Here, the invitation of grief is not to return to life as it was before, but to *make music with what remains*.

In Chapter 2, I think about the 'wound' of our *mortality*, which is a necessary loss[1] we experience as we relinquish the illusion that we will live for ever. Although we cannot easily contemplate our own deaths, I consider the ancient wisdom that insists that *remembering death enhances life*.

In Chapter 3, I think about the grief of increasing *dependence*, whether through illness, ageing, progressive disability or dying. Our loss of independence and autonomy asks to be mourned. Yet, even in the confinement and diminishment of these conditions, we may encounter more of our true value and creativity. I consider the possibility that there may be a worthwhile life to be lived, *just as I am*.

A fourth and necessary loss is *parting*, which is an inevitable experience as we grow up or move on from places and people. In the grief of parting lies an invitation to make courageous choices, particularly for those who are left behind. I pick up on the insight that *love is proved in the letting go*.

I shift the focus in Chapter 5 to consider *nostalgia*, a 'sweet sorrow' that we almost enjoy. I suggest the grief of nostalgia

xv

may be less about trying to recover the past and more to do with a need *to tend neglected parts of ourselves* or to search for an ultimate home.

In Chapter 6, *failure* comes into view. We all fail in something at some point in our lives; but our experience of failure often differs. This chapter looks at how we frame this loss, and whether there are more constructive meanings that we can give to it. I explore the rich possibility that *failure is an option.*

Chapter 7 examines *shame*: in particular, the shame that arises when grief must remain hidden. Shame obstructs connection and growth; but an honest naming of our private grief can begin a journey towards wholeness. I go in search of *the grief that dares to speak its name.*

In Chapter 8, I visit the 'fork in the road' of *regret*. Making choices in life is unavoidable. Occasionally, we each look back and regret the path we took, mourning the unchosen path and the unlived life it represents. Regret puts us more in touch with the life each of us has chosen and invites us *to be present to our one and only life.*

In the last chapter, I turn to consider a different kind of loss altogether: *forgetting*. This is the loss of parts of our humanity through an act of collective amnesia. We in the West have largely lost touch with our shared experience of the sacred; we have forgotten that we are animal bodies embedded in the natural world. We suffer from barely recognized nature grief and soul grief. By unearthing our collective grief, we can *remember our roots in soil and soul.*

All is not loss?

Two threads run though these chapters. One is the observation that *loss is all pervasive*; the other is the paradoxical possibility that *all is not loss*. These raise a couple of questions: is the loss we encounter at every turn merely an occupational hazard of being human? Might our frequent losses nurture the seeds of spiritual transformation?

INTRODUCTION: THE SPIRITUALITY OF GRIEF

From the outset, we do have to take seriously the possibility that human life is a story of repeated loss, with no redemptive arc. We are not born into the world clutching a guarantee that the pain that lies ahead will somehow be worth it. In this view, there is no ultimate purpose to human life, but simply a causal chain of events stretching blindly back and forward in time. Beyond our ability to reproduce and nurture the next generation, the universe doesn't care whether we live or die, thrive or suffer.

Even with this view, however, we can remain curious about the litany of loss that life brings. From the standpoint of a Darwinian rationalist, the prevalence of suffering, decay and death in the world of living things invites questions. The anthropologist Roy Rappaport has suggested that 'anything universal to human culture is likely to contribute to human survival'.[2] This is an intriguing possibility that might make us wonder whether, even in a blind universe, loss could have an adaptive function for the species.

The prevalence of loss raises further questions for the spiritually minded. Is loss simply an awkward fact of a fallen world? Is it the doleful evidence of the brokenness of things? Is it an inconvenient interruption in the smooth flow of our heaven-blessed lives? Does it feel like a pointless waste: a landfill heap of failures, regrets and broken relationships?

Or is there more to it than this? If loss is an integral part of what it means to be human, the question remains: how does it fit into the whole? What if loss might also mean gain? This book is an attempt to plumb this question. My hunch, of course, is that loss may give back in some surprising ways, even as we grieve it. In short, there is a *spirituality* to grief that emerges from these two truths: *loss is all pervasive; all is not loss.*

Blind alleys

Immediately we suggest that loss could in some way be redemptive, I begin to hear alarm bells. It is too easy to be glib around suffering. In setting out this 'hunch', then, let me be clear. There are several popular responses to grief I will not be advancing. I call them 'blind alley' responses precisely because they lead nowhere. In fact, often they are harmful.

One of these is the idea that *every cloud has a silver lining*. The tell-tale words that often begin such responses are 'At least …': 'At least your father lived a long life' or 'At least you still have your mother.' We can be quick to respond to the pain of loss in these sing-song tones, but such toxic positivity fails to square up to the pain of loss; it fails to acknowledge it and to name it. Although I have heard it played at funerals, I will not be humming Monty Python's 'Always Look on the Bright Side of Life'.

Another popular response to grieving people is to try to encourage them with how well they are doing. Although meant kindly, it rewards people for being 'strong' and for moving on quickly. I suspect it may often be more about the speaker's need for the grieving person to hide the messy business of grief. We see versions of this muscular grieving from funeral poems to fridge magnets. Nietzsche's aphorism sums it up well: *what doesn't kill you, makes you stronger*. (An unfortunate motto for the fridge door.) But loss and grief are not part of some celestial boot camp, intended to toughen us up in double-quick time. If grief is transforming, it needs light and space to grow and, above all, time. For some, the fruit of grieving may never ripen.

Another viral meme I will avoid is *everything happens for a reason*. This piece of fatalism is comforting until we are confronted with serious loss or tragedy; at that point, the 'reason' becomes somewhat elusive. In Scotland, where I live, it has a popular equivalent, frequently quoted, and even framed on the wall of my local pub: *whit's fur ye'll no go past ye*. In other words, if it's destined for you, it will happen. This may be a comforting thought when you nearly missed out on a university place, but somewhat scary if a scythe-wielding silhouette should appear on the horizon.

I sometimes wonder why we are so tongue-tied with the grieving. Is it because we reach for these kinds of stock phrases,

INTRODUCTION: THE SPIRITUALITY OF GRIEF

then realize that, in the face of the acute pain of grief, these words simply don't work? In writing this book, I am conscious that you may be a reader experiencing the intense pain of acute grief. I hope you will feel that your grief is taken seriously, and that you don't find any such glib or 'blind alley' responses.

A word about stories

Throughout this book, I tell stories to illustrate my argument. Any stories that appear to be about people with whom I have worked pastorally or therapeutically are *fictional composites*: that is, they are made-up stories based on themes or principles I have observed in 35 years of doing pastoral work. If you recognize something of yourself in any of these stories, be assured that I am not telling *your* story – except in the sense that your experience may be similar to that of many grieving people. Although every person's grief is unique, grief shares some common features. Indeed, for many grieving people, it is the discovery that they are not alone in their grief that can help to orient them. And if, as this book suggests, we are all grieving pervasive loss, then these stories are *our stories* – the stories of how we love and lose; the stories of what it means to be human.

I write from a particular context, which I think it is important to acknowledge. I am a white, middle-class, middle-aged man, living in Scotland. Many of my examples come, unashamedly, from a Scottish context. In part, this is a pragmatic choice: 'Write what you know' is the common advice to authors. But it is also a conscious choice, acknowledging that all perspectives emerge from *some* context or other. The literati of Islington are no less (or more) parochial than the Orkney poets. Recognizing that all authors are situated somewhere, I happily write from *my* centre. In doing so, I acknowledge I am no less immune to the myopia and prejudices of my social and geographical location than any other writer.

In what follows, I will ask the question, 'What's spiritual about grief?' It is important to hammer out a working definition of 'spirituality', as the word itself can be used so broadly as to become almost meaningless. If chiselling away at definitions does not excite you, feel free to skip the rest of this introduction. The important thing to carry with you through the book is that I will be using a working definition of spirituality as that which fosters *connection, insight and growth*. The spirituality of grief is encountered in those moments where these outcomes – despite all odds – emerge in the midst of our grieving.

What's spiritual about grief?

As we have noted, one of the challenges of speaking about spirituality is that the term can be so broad as to be almost meaningless. It is in danger of referring to everything or nothing. Yet, like 'religion' or 'culture' – words that have a broad semantic range – 'spirituality' is a word we cannot easily do without. If we are to explore the *spirituality* of grieving, we have to look at definitions. I will not attempt to arrive at *the* definition of spirituality; I will simply aim to be as clear as I can about how I intend to use the term.

The idea of the 'spiritual'

The word 'spirituality' is a relatively recent term – a noun that stands on the shoulders of the much older adjective, 'spiritual'. This word has undergone a series of transformations, often being defined by what it is not. If we look at the history of the word in Christian thought, for example, we find St Paul, in his first-century letters, contrasting the spiritual with the *carnal*, the unholy impulse in humans that leads them away from the things of the Spirit. By the third century, the meaning alters, so that the spiritual (soul) comes to be set against the *material* (body), under the influence of Platonism. Later, in medieval Europe, this spiritual/material division shifts to being applied at a societal level, defining the realm of the spiritual against

INTRODUCTION: THE SPIRITUALITY OF GRIEF

that of the *temporal*. We see the legacy of this distinction in the UK House of Lords, between the 'Lords Temporal' and the 'Lords Spiritual' (the Anglican bishops). In the late medieval period, the English word 'spirituality' begins to creep into the language as a noun referring to the clergy or their jurisdictions, in contrast to the 'temporalities' or the things belonging to the everyday material world. Hence, by the eve of the European Reformation, the 'spiritual' is defined in contrast (successively) to the carnal, the material and the temporal.

In the sixteenth century, the word mutates again, under the influence of Ignatius of Loyola (the founder of the Jesuits, called the first psychologist). His immensely influential *Spiritual Exercises* recast the 'spiritual' as the realm of the *interior life* by paying close attention to feelings and imagination as sites at which God comes to meet us. This change brings us much closer to our modern conception of the 'spiritual' as belonging to the inner, subjective life, in contrast to the external world of religious institutions, their doctrines and liturgies.

A final shift, which takes place only in the second half of the twentieth century, is the mutation of the 'spiritual' from the realm of the collective to that of the *individual*. This involves the 'spiritual' breaking out from under the umbrella of religious institutions and being embraced as a realm of human experience. It enables the popular description of being 'spiritual but not religious' to emerge. Although there have been attempts to create forms of corporate gathering around this identity, it remains essentially an individual identity choice. To add, then, to the pre-Reformation mutations of the word, we can see 'spiritual' being defined in contrast, first, to the external and then to the institutional.

The emergence of 'spirituality'

Woven around these changes, the word 'spirituality' has emerged. As a noun, its meaning has followed the meandering contours of its older adjective 'spiritual'. As we have seen, it once referred to the domain of the clergy. Its French equivalent, *spiritualité*, was perhaps the first use of the term to refer to interior, mystical or ascetical devotion. Here, it was used negatively, as a criticism of the seventeenth-century Quietists. In the two centuries following, it lost its negative associations and came to describe the different approaches to inner piety in religious life.[3]

It is only in the twentieth century that the English word *spirituality* comes to refer to the inner life of devotion. The means by which faith traditions foster this inner life becomes a subject of historical research, and it becomes commonplace to refer to spirituality as a quality of a religious tradition: to speak of 'Catholic spirituality', 'Quaker spirituality', and so on.

From here, it is a short step to the secularizing and individualizing of the term. William James, in his influential *Varieties of Religious Experience* (originally published in 1902), defines religion as *'the feelings, acts, and experiences of individual men in their solitude, so far as they apprehend themselves to stand in relation to whatever they may consider the divine'*.[4] This is a definition that brackets off individual spirituality from institutional religion. A further impetus to the individualizing of spirituality comes with the anti-institutional mood of the 1960s and the 'turn to the subjective'. For the counterculture, spirituality becomes a personal project, with western seekers appropriating eastern spiritual paths and emphasizing holistic spiritual practices and humanistic values. By the twenty-first century, much of the counterculture has become mainstream, so that values and practices that seemed radical in the 1960s are now standard in many sectors. The wholesale adoption of mindfulness techniques as a form of secular meditation is one example of this.

The individualizing and secularizing of 'spirituality' has led us to today's broad-brush understandings of the term. Abbot Christopher Jamison has characterized contemporary spirituality as 'psychological well-being combined with the moral golden rule'.[5] Others have defined it loosely as 'anything that

INTRODUCTION: THE SPIRITUALITY OF GRIEF

[seems] to enhance the sense of the sacred in human life'[6] or 'that which succeeds in bringing one to inner transformation'.[7] Definitions of spirituality are legion, which makes it hard to use the word with any precision.

If we are to think about the spirituality of grief, however, it is important that we have some clarity. Looking back at the development of the term, it seems evident that historic understandings of the 'spiritual' in opposition to the *carnal*, the *material* and the *temporal* won't do. To contemporary ears, it would seem a strange definition of spirituality that excluded the 'flesh' and its desires, the material world, and the human stage in time and space.

Common themes

Although there is no consensus about the term, there are common approaches and themes. One approach is to understand spirituality not by what it *is* but by what it *does*: a so-called 'functional definition'. The advantage of this is that it frees us from trying to define an elusive essence to spirituality and enables us to sketch its outline in terms of outcomes. Spirituality may be known by its fruit.

Brené Brown has been one of the most influential writers and researchers in the realm of psychology and management in recent decades. In the data she collected for her book *Rising Strong*, a picture of spirituality emerges, which she comes to define as

> recognizing and celebrating that we are all inextricably connected to one another by a power greater than all of us, and that our connection to that power and to one another is grounded in love and belonging. Practicing spirituality brings a sense of perspective, meaning, and purpose to our lives.[8]

Some key themes that emerge from this definition are connection, the values of love and compassion, and the gaining of perspective and insight.

Similarly, in a paper for the Royal College of Psychiatrists, Dr Maya Spencer has sketched an outline of spirituality that includes an awareness of the 'greater whole', our significance and purpose in this, and an aspiration to develop mature values.[9]

Another example comes from the National Health Service in Scotland, where I worked as a health-care chaplain for a number of years. The Scottish Government published its *National Framework* for spiritual care in 2023; it defines spirituality as the part of us that 'seeks to discover meaning, purpose and hope in those aspects of our experience that matter most to us' and that informs our personal values. It acknowledges that people are more than bodies that need fixing and cites research indicating that spirituality 'can help people maintain health and cope with illness, trauma, loss, and life transitions by integrating body, mind and spirit'.[10] Here again, we touch on the themes of holistic connection, meaning, purpose and growth in values.

These examples could be multiplied. What matters for our purpose here is that we have a clear-enough working definition of spirituality that broadly reflects the way the word is commonly used.

As the examples above indicate, there are three outcomes, in particular, that occur repeatedly in contemporary discussions of spirituality. In brief, spirituality is that which fosters *connection, insight and growth*. Spirituality nurtures holistic connection – to our inner selves, to one another, to our environment and to the transcendent; it joins the dots of our disparate experiences and helps us to weave them into a meaningful whole; and it shapes our values and helps to form us into people of maturity and integrity.

INTRODUCTION: THE SPIRITUALITY OF GRIEF

The religious and the spiritual

This working definition is intended to be useful to those who situate their spirituality within a historic religious tradition and to those who don't. If you belong to the former group, you might understand spirituality to be primarily to do with the mood and mode of worship; you might also be familiar with the way it mediates between the institutional and personal dimensions of faith. If so, my definition may seem too broad. Yet the themes of connection, insight and growth have direct counterparts in traditional religious language, in terms such as 'prayer', 'wisdom' and 'obedience'. For those who, by contrast, are 'spiritual but not religious' or simply curious, I aim to speak about the spirituality of grief in ways that make no assumptions about religious belief or belonging. There are, of course, important resources within historic faith traditions that address our grief. For example, if we believe there is a life after death, and a personal God who walks with us in our pain, this might transform our grieving. Here, however, I will not be exploring this wealth of resources because they depend on a prior faith commitment. The pastoral wisdom of the major world faiths is beyond the scope of this book.

When grief is raw

Readers may be at different stages in a journey of grief. In the early stages of acute grief, it may not be possible to entertain the kinds of reflections in this book. It may even feel like an outrage to suggest there can be a 'spirituality' to something so painful as grief. One of the common burdens borne by those who suffer acute grief is the expectation of others that they will somehow be 'over it' soon. Yet, there is no timetable to grieving; and, for many, their experience is not so much that they 'get over' their loss, but that it becomes transformed, slowly, into a less painful burden.

The psychotherapist Francis Weller recounts talking to a group about bereavement when a man in his 70s asked him how he could get over his sadness. Weller replied:

> I can't accept the premise of your question. It implies an ending to your grief. I don't think it will end. It will soften over time and turn into a tender melancholy. In fact, your grief is your new relationship with your wife. It will be the ongoing reminder of your love and your life together. This sadness keeps her in your world.[11]

We often think of grief in relation to bereavement, which is potentially one of the most painful experiences a human can endure. But grief has many forms, as I've said, some of which I explore in this book. This is not a book 'about' bereavement, although the first chapter will explore this aspect of loss. Feel free to come back to it later. If the notion that grieving can hold an invitation to spiritual growth seems impossible, perhaps you would prefer to wait to hear its call first-hand. After all, one of the joys of books is that you can always put them down.

Notes

1 See J. Viorst, 1986, *Necessary Losses*, New York: Simon & Schuster, for a helpful exploration of losses that come as an unavoidable part of human experience.

2 R. A. Rappaport, 'The Sacred in Human Evolution', *Annual Review of Ecology and Systematics*, 2 (1971), pp. 23–44, at https://www.jstor.org/stable/2096920, accessed 14.04.2025.

3 Cheslyn Jones, Geoffrey Wainwright and Edward Yarnold, 1994, *The Study of Spirituality*, London: SPCK.

4 W. James, 2002, *Varieties of Religious Experience: A study in human nature*, London: Routledge, pp. 29–30.

5 C. Jamison, 2009, *Finding Sanctuary: Monastic steps for everyday life*, Collegeville, MN: Liturgical Press, p. 143.

6 P. Young-Eisendrath and M. E. Miller, 2005, *The Psychology of Mature Spirituality: Integrity, wisdom, transcendence*, London: Routledge, p. 3.

INTRODUCTION: THE SPIRITUALITY OF GRIEF

7 Anthony de Mello, 1984, *The Song of the Bird*, Garden City, NY: Image Books, p. 11.

8 B. Brown, 2015, *Rising Strong*, London: Penguin, p. 10.

9 M. Spencer, 2012, *What Is Spirituality? A personal exploration*, Royal College of Psychiatrists, at https://www.rcpsych.ac.uk/docs/default-source/members/sigs/spirituality-spsig/what-is-spirituality-maya-spencer-x.pdf, accessed 14.04.2025.

10 Scottish Government, 2023, 'Discovering Meaning, Purpose and Hope through Person Centred Well-Being and Spiritual Care: A national framework', at https://www.gov.scot/publications/discovering-meaning-purpose-hope-through-person-centred-well-being-spiritual-care-national-framework, accessed 14.04.2025.

11 F. Weller, 2015, *The Wild Edge of Sorrow: Rituals of renewal and the sacred work of grief*, Berkeley, CA: North Atlantic Books, p. 122.

1

Bereavement

> Our job is to make music with what remains.
> (Itzhak Perlman)[1]

Perhaps the most profound grief human beings can experience is the death of someone we love. Sometimes a death is expected and comes peacefully enough at the end of a long and fruitful life. At other times, a death may feel like a tragedy. A husband collapses. A child dies by suicide. A mother of young children develops a terminal illness. A friend is killed on the road. Whichever way, a bereavement can leave us feeling that our lives have come to a halt: there is little point in going on with life. We may believe that we will never recover our loved one; we may never recover ourselves.

In grief, W. H. Auden cried out for the clock to be stopped. And as our clock stops, it can seem impossible that, for others, life goes on. One bereaved widow, whose husband died at the beginning of the COVID 19 lockdown, commented that she was comforted by the lockdown: the world *had* stopped with her. In grief, we lose our sense of the passage of time: one part of us can hardly believe that so many months have passed since the death – for months we have survived (but how?); another part of us experiences the death as only yesterday or this morning. As a bereaved father put it: 'Our lives are stuck on that November day when the policeman knocked on the door.'

Death can leave us feeling robbed. At the heart of the word 'bereaved' is an Old English verb meaning to plunder – a term preserved in Scots as *reive*. We still meet it in the phrase 'the Border Reivers': ruthless families who raided one another across the Anglo-Scottish border in the late medieval period. Like the Reivers, death can feel similar to an enemy from a foreign country that has come to wreck and pillage.

Bereavement can overwhelm us. We can feel engulfed by an incendiary cocktail of feelings: sadness, guilt, helplessness, shame, stress, anxiety, lostness, emptiness, numbness, disbelief. Some describe feeling as if they have lost a limb, which continues to send them phantom pain. Sometimes the death itself is traumatic, even if the circumstances are not; the pain of grief is compounded by the horror of final memories. One young man commented, 'I never realized someone could look so much like death before they died.'

Grief has been described as a journey without a destination. We continually under-estimate the length of that journey: how long it will take us to navigate the hardscrabble territory of grief in the faint hope that one day we may reach some more liveable plain. As I listen to stories of recent bereavement, I feel like an innkeeper at the start of that arduous journey; my heart goes out to those who have no choice but to embark upon it. For many, I am conscious of a long road ahead of them. There are few maps, and few now subscribe to the notion that there are 'stages of grief'.[2] What Cariad Lloyd calls the 'grief-mess' seems a more appropriate description of grief's itinerary. 'Grief is a huge, swirling, tangled ball of wires – like the worst headphone knot you have ever seen.'[3] There is no neat progression. 'Grief, when it comes, is nothing we expect it to be,' observes Joan Didion. 'Grief is different. Grief has no distance. Grief comes in waves, paroxysms, sudden apprehensions that weaken the knees and blind the eyes and obliterate the dailiness of life.'[4]

Grief can be isolating. While friends and relatives often get back to their lives quickly after a death, those closest to the person who has died may find themselves alone with the enormity of their feelings, and few people to talk to about them. Conventional expectations might be that a person will get back to some kind of normality after a few months. Even the 'bible' of American psychiatry – the *DSM-5-TR* – diagnoses acute grief, lasting more than a year, as a disorder.[5]

BEREAVEMENT

This is a recent change that has not been without its critics. For many, however, the reality is that it can be years before they feel they are back on an even keel. Indeed, there is a view that we never recover, only adapt. Grieving has not gone wrong: it has simply gone on.

In the face of grief, we find ways to adjust the pain, turning the tap down to a trickle, or even off for a while. We avoid reminders of the person: places, pictures, songs. We drive home the long way round. We go on holiday with friends, pressing the 'mute' button on our grief until we return, perhaps to an empty house. Our mind plays tricks: we wake in the morning and, for a second, believe our loved one is still here. We try to forget, and we fear forgetting. Or we buy flowers, only remembering as we reach her doorstep.

The psychotherapist Irvin Yalom describes hearing that a local bookshop was displaying copies of both his and his wife's books. Delighted, he stopped there with his iPhone in hand to take a picture to show her. Only *then* did he remember: 'Marilyn is dead.'[6]

At the same time as avoiding reality, we may try to keep the person close, clinging to external symbols: a husband's glasses lie untouched on the bedside table; a mother's bed linen remains unwashed; a daughter bags her mother's clothes to preserve their smell; a husband speaks to his wife's ashes. We talk to the robin in the garden and take comfort that our partner is listening. We visit the grave. Joan Didion could not bear to part with her late husband's shoes, she realized, because of course he would need them when he returned.

Grief racks our bodies as well as our souls. The musician Nick Cave described how, after the death of his teenage son, he was 'filled with an internal chaos, a roaring physical feeling in my very being ... I could feel it literally rushing through my body and bursting out the ends of my fingers.'[7] We may experience pains in our body, just where our loved one did before the diagnosis. We may feel that we ourselves have not got long to live. 'We tend to see grief as an emotional state,' Cave observed, 'but it is also an atrocious destabilizing assault upon the body. So much so that it can feel terminal.'[8] Colin Murray Parkes, in his seminal study on bereavement, wrote that 'grief resembles a physical injury more closely than any other type of illness'.[9]

The spirituality of bereavement

These are mere sketches of bereavement, but they are, perhaps, enough to put us in touch with its intensity. In the face of such loss, can it make any sense to ask if there is a 'spirituality of grief'? Is it not cruel, or absurd, to ask how the experience of acute grief could foster greater connection, insight or growth? Yet what makes the question at least admissible are the testimonies of those who have experienced great tragedies and have emerged in a world both racked with grief and strangely enlarged. For some, just surviving the bereavement may feel like growth. Alison Wertheimer concludes her study of the experiences of people bereaved by suicide with a modest hope: 'survival is possible'.[10]

As I said in the introduction, finding a spiritual dimension to bereavement is not about looking for silver linings on dark clouds. Rather, it is about asking whether there is a voice in the darkness itself that issues a quiet invitation to something more: a thought that Nick Cave calls 'the idea of grief as a gift'. The loss of a child is surely one of the most painful bereavements; yet Cave found himself able to touch on its wild potential: 'Grief as a positive force. Grief that can become, if we allow it its full expression, a defiant, sometimes mutinous energy.'[11] 'We are remade in times of grief,' wrote Francis Weller, 'broken apart and reassembled.'[12]

How, then, might the grief of bereavement speak a quiet invitation to a more holistic connection with others, the environment and the realm of the transcendent? What new ways of seeing might it open up to us? How might it nudge us to realign our values? In short, how might we encounter the spirituality of bereavement?

Recovering self

It is common for bereaved people to feel lost. I often hear something such as this: 'I don't know where I am any more.' It is as if all landmarks have vanished, all direction gone, and the map we were holding has been torn from our hands. As W. H. Auden intimated in his 'Funeral Blues', losing a loved one can feel like losing our compass altogether: the person from whom we took our bearings has gone.

But there is something else people say that has often intrigued me: 'I don't know *who* I am any more.' Grief can eat away at our sense of identity.

Who am I now?

Losing ourselves can be partly to do with losing our role. The wife is no longer a wife; the parent is no longer a parent; the daughter is no longer a carer. 'About a week after my partner died,' one man commented, 'I was struck with the sudden realization that I am now a single person.' After the death of his wife, Irvin Yalom came to a shocking realization: 'I astonish myself and I keep repeating it: *I have never lived as an independent adult.*'[13]

The death of someone close, often a partner or a spouse, can raise another sort of question: 'Who was I before I met this person?' Choosing a life partner often involves some compromise; parts of the self that might otherwise have emerged may be muted in favour of those that serve the relationship. We suppress our inner traveller, socialite, aesthete, naturalist or whatever else is not easily shared. The death of a partner can reawaken these slumbering parts of the self.

For some, the compromise has been unequal: a wife who has followed her military or diplomat husband around the world, for example, may have had little agency to develop her own interests. Or a woman who has lived for decades with an abusive partner may find the freedom of bereavement overwhelming. Grief, here, can be complex: as well as grieving for the dead person, the woman must grieve for the life she didn't have, and the parts of herself that were denied or denigrated.

Likewise, people who have found themselves locked into caring roles may also emerge, post-bereavement, uncertain about their status in life. Others may feel still bound to their partners, wanting to take forward the lives of the deceased, particularly when they have been cut short. In death, our loved ones may continue to influence our roles in life.

The question 'Who am I now?' is itself a kind of invitation. As a family rebalances after a death, its members have an opportunity to decide for themselves. It may be a time to resist the expectations of family members, perhaps by refusing to fill the shoes of the deceased. The death of a parent may expose the fault-lines between siblings and lead them to re-evaluate what matters to them. Others may rediscover parts of themselves that were overshadowed or disallowed by their partners. I think of one woman who went to work for a charity in Kenya after her husband died, and another who started an antiques business. Neither felt that they had 'permission' to do these things before.

The voice of this invitation may be quiet at first. For months or years after a major loss, the keening cry within may drown out all other sounds as we search for our loved ones. The world feels empty, barren, pointless. When we do hear a whisper on the wind, it can be tempting to dismiss it. We can't recover our loved ones; but any attempt to recover the *self* feels like a betrayal and it may take some time before we can each hear the voice for ourselves.

Beyond anxiety, guilt and loneliness

Another way in which grief might invite us to grow is to move us through the powerful feelings of anxiety, guilt and loneliness that often accompany bereavement.

Anxiety is common, especially when we depended in some way on the people we have lost. Individuals often describe feeling like little girls or boys again after a loss. The thought of reinvesting in life, on our own, may seem too frightening. It can feel safer to set up a vigil by the grave, like the heroic little dog Greyfriars Bobby, immortalized in a bronze statue in Edinburgh. When his master died in 1858, Bobby reputedly kept watch for 14 years by the grave in Greyfriars Kirkyard.

Cave observes that 'there can be a kind of morbid worshipping of an absence. A reluctance to move beyond the trauma, *because the trauma is where the one you lost resides*, and therefore the place where meaning exists.'[14] Setting up camp by the graveside makes emotional sense, when it feels there is nowhere else you would rather be. Yet endless searching and watching may prevent us hearing grief's patient invitation to keep living.

Guilt is another powerful feeling we must reckon with. In my work with bereaved people, I have noticed how often guilt accompanies bereavement. This experience is so common, in fact, that I sometimes describe guilt as an 'occupational hazard' of being bereaved. People can feel that they failed to protect their loved one from pain; failed to advocate for them in hospital; failed to get them home; failed to make amends; failed to have a final conversation; failed to give them their last wishes; failed to get the funeral right; failed to be there at the end. At one level, we know we're not to blame; but no amount of logic can touch the feeling. The journalist John Humphrys noted, after the death of his father, that 'the guilt may be entirely irrational, but grief and reason are not natural bedfellows'.[15]

Often, just beneath the guilt, there is a feeling of helplessness. For some, it may be less frightening to think that they failed to do something within their power than to accept that there was really nothing they could have done.

Guilt can be particularly prevalent after the loss of an ambivalent relationship. It can be hard to acknowledge the hate, as well as the love, we had for the deceased. In Freud's language, the sadistic impulses we had towards the person become turned inward, in self-reproach and the self-torment of guilt and 'melancholia'.[16] Unable to bear what Melanie Klein called our 'triumph' over the dead,[17] we turn our aggressive impulses against the self.

Guilt roars: grief whispers. Guilt takes us back through the story and itemizes what we got wrong. Grief invites us to acknowledge our mixed feelings towards the person who has died and extend compassion to ourselves. Julia Samuel suggests: 'Writing down conflicting messages – for example, feeling both relieved and sad about a death – enables us to see what we are telling ourselves, thereby illuminating what is going on inside.'[18] As we sort out our feelings, we become better able to reappraise the circumstances of the death and carry a more realistic memory of the person within. This in turn may enable us to dispense with some of the irrational guilt we feel.

Loneliness, too, can add to the burden of grief. When a loved one dies, we lose a unique relationship. How can we ever communicate what we have lost? And for a partner or an only child, there may be no one else who shares the magnitude of our loss. The pain of repeatedly returning to an empty house can be excruciating. Bereavement isolates us further when those around us withdraw, unsure of how to respond. Parkes points to anthropological studies in which the bereaved are treated as if tainted, unlucky or toxic.[19] C. S. Lewis said, 'I'm aware of being an embarrassment to everyone I meet.'[20] The common complaint of the single widow is that she is no longer included on the guest list.

Grief may also cause us to withdraw from others. Kind friends may try to be helpful by inviting us on holiday or including us in social occasions. While some find this helpful, others feel anxious and overwhelmed in company. Those experiencing acute grief can feel as if they are watching the party from behind a glass screen. They may wear a smile but, inside, they feel no joy from being with others and typically want to get away as soon as possible.

John Bowlby writes that 'intimate attachments to other human beings are the hub around which a person's life revolves' and that 'from these a person draws his strength and enjoyment of life'.[21] In grief, these can be torn away. It can feel as if we will never laugh again. In the midst of such crippling feelings of isolation, how can grief ever foster connection? Surviving a significant bereavement and learning to thrive and love again may not come about by returning to the social world we enjoyed before. The people we thought were friends have been tested: some have been found wanting; others have stepped forward and surprised us. Bereavement may leave our table empty, but not for ever. Connection is possible because grief may beckon to others from the back door. If, as Bowlby indicates, we are wired for intimacy, our spiritual recovery will involve finding others who allow us to *be*, just as we are, now.

When we are first bereaved, the idea of 'moving on' can seem impossible; unthinkable, even. Perhaps we literally 'forget' ourselves by not eating properly, washing or sleeping. Typically, over time, we learn to pay more attention to our own needs. Eventually, we can begin to contemplate our future and connect more fully with the self: 'Who am I now? Can I make it on my own? What will I carry with me? What can I leave behind?'

Recovering the other

As well as inviting us to recover ourselves, grief carries an invitation to recover the other. Mourning can be described as the paradoxical process of finding a way to carry our loved one within us, while we learn to move on without them. Although death separates us from the physical person, we experience an enduring sense of their continuing reality within. There is no adequate word in English to name the ongoing felt presence of a person we have internalized but no longer see; yet our relationship with this inner presence lies at the heart of bereavement.[22] Just as grief can connect us more to the self, it can also connect us to the other – to the person who has died – in ways that are less raw and 'wrenching'[23] than we experienced at first.

In trying to describe this process, various 'models' of grief have emerged. Like the parts of the elephant in the Indian fable of the blind men and the elephant, each emphasizes a different part of the experience. In one model, grieving a loved one is like a *see-saw*, which oscillates between attempting to recover the loved one and trying to move on oneself. Another describes an expanding *doughnut*, in which the 'hole' in the centre represents the loss: the hole does not diminish in size, but the bereaved person learns to build a new life around it. Still another model sees grief as a *task-list* to work through, until mourning is complete and the bereaved person can move on. Other models picture a *journey*: grief is a territory that mourners will move through in 'phases', although they might wander in circles at times. A further model imagines an invisible *thread* connecting the mourners with the deceased, where the process of mourning is about finding realistic ways to maintain that bond.[24]

What is common to many of these models is a shift from seeking the deceased 'out there' to finding and carrying them 'in here'. As J. William Worden puts it, our task is 'to emotionally relocate the deceased and move on with life'.[25] If grief invites us to connect in a new way with ourselves, it also invites us to find a new connection with our loved ones.

Grief is like growing up

It was one of John Bowlby's great achievements to highlight the importance of our early attachment to a secure parental figure for our psychological well-being in later life. Together with Bowlby, a fellow psychiatrist, Colin Murray Parkes, came to see that adult bereavement mirrored the experience of a child's separation from a parent and that many grief reactions were similar in both situations: 'I think it fair to say that the pining or yearning that constitutes separation anxiety is the characteristic feature of the pang of grief.'[26] A child learns to be comfortably alone when they have internalized a sense of their main carer's ongoing presence, such as an image of a parent, say, that they carry within. As we have seen, something similar happens in grieving: we learn to carry the image of our loved one internally and cease the search for them 'out there'. We maintain a sense that, in some way, they have a continuing presence. This might be a belief that they are now in a 'better place' or their spirit endures somewhere; it may be simply that they remain vivid in our memories and are 'held in our hearts'.

Paradoxically, then, grief can connect us to our loved ones in a new way, in the wake of a loss that can feel as if all bonds have been broken. These 'continuing bonds'[27] can come as a surprise. C. S. Lewis feared forgetting his wife after she died. Later, unbidden, he found himself encountering 'an unobtrusive but massive sense that she is, just as much as ever, a fact to be taken into account'.[28] This shift may be gradual or sudden. A friend who lost his fiancée in an accident described to me how, ten years later, he had a surprising realization: all those years he had been carrying a painful sense of her absence; now he could see that he could carry her with him as a *presence*. In that moment, he sensed her smiling, as if she were saying, 'That took you a while!'

Surprised by empathy

Grief can connect us in other ways, too. For some, being confronted with the precariousness of life opens up greater empathy. For Nick Cave, the death of his son put him in touch with the fact that humans are all vulnerable and 'imperilled': 'And because of that, I feel a kind of empathy with people I have never felt before. It feels urgent and new and fundamental.'[29] Alison Wertheimer observed that some survivors of suicide 'talked of becoming "more compassionate", of "being more aware of other people's feelings", and of "realizing that other people are vulnerable"'.[30] People who have lost a loved one to cancer sometimes report now 'seeing cancer everywhere', and finding in themselves a deep compassion and empathy for others. Robert Romanyshyn describes that, in the early moments of grief, 'I was in a ghost world, and my sense of isolation was almost total.' Yet,

> the long, slow winter of mourning dissolved that separateness in unexpected ways ... In these moments, I have felt myself attached to others with a compassion I have not known before and drawn, too, beyond myself to the green brilliance of the world.[31]

Grief can open us to the transcendent

Spirituality stitches together the fabric of our experience into a meaningful garment. As we have seen, one way this happens is by connecting us more fully to ourselves, to others and to the environment, so that we experience the world more holistically. But what of the inner, or upward, connection to the realm of the transcendent? How might the spirituality of grief bring us closer to God or the non-material world?

Modern thinkers who have reflected deeply on the nature of death have often tended to view the spiritual quest with suspicion. Freud dismissed our belief in a benevolent 'Providence' protecting us from the 'pitiless forces of nature'.[32] Instead, he viewed our religious impulses as responses to our infantile helplessness in the face of life's dangers and, not least, the prospect of death. Others have seen faith in an afterlife as a kind of magical thinking that protects us from our own death anxiety and keeps alive the hope of reunion. After the death of his wife, the psychotherapist Irvin Yalom reflected on his curious wish to be buried alongside her in the same coffin: 'I, an ardent materialist, jettison my reason and bask unashamedly in the entirely fantastical thought that if you and I were in the same coffin, then we'd be together for all time.'[33] After the death of her husband, Joan Didion noted: 'I did not believe in the resurrection of the body but I still believed that given the right circumstances he would come back.'[34]

Others may discern in grief an invitation to look beyond – inward or upward – to connect with someone (or something) greater than themselves, and will take this invitation seriously. True: faith can founder on the rocks of bereavement; but, for some, grief strips away the theatre props and stage flats of everyday life and reveals something essential.

People who are dying may see things more clearly; frequently, they exhort the rest of us to treasure the life we have. Bereaved people, likewise, can emerge from the fog of numbness and shock, from the burden of pain, and find that their grieving can be transformative. They may develop a capacity to see the world at depth, to sift what matters and to reach for essential truths. Once again, Nick Cave captures something of this potential for transformation:

> perhaps grief can be seen as a kind of exalted state where the person who is grieving is the closest they will ever be to the fundamental essence of things. Because, in grief, you become deeply acquainted with the idea of human mortality ... As far as I can see there is a transformative aspect to this place of suffering. We are essentially altered or remade by it. This process is terrifying ... Everything seems so fragile and precious ... It actually feels like grief and God are somehow intertwined.[35]

The vocational call of grief

If there is a spiritual dimension to the loss of bereavement, then it will ultimately issue in a renewed vocational call. We have seen how grief can connect us more to ourselves, to others and to the transcendent, helping us to 'see the world at depth'. At first, it may be enough just to heed the call to survive. Yet loss may call us further: to encounter the 'transformative aspect to this place of suffering'; to be 'altered or remade by it'.

There is a story told of the accomplished violinist Itzhak Perlman arriving on stage to play a violin concerto. He walked forward on crutches, because he had contracted polio at the age of four, and sat down to play, as he always did. As he tuned his instrument, there was an audible crack: one of his four strings had broken. Despite this, he signalled to the conductor to begin and played the concerto on the remaining three strings. At the end of the concert, he rose to speak. 'Our job', he said, 'is to make music with what remains.'

There is a truth here that could apply to all kinds of loss, but it has a particular resonance for dying and bereavement. I was introduced to this story by a wise and experienced health-care chaplain on my team, when I worked for the Spiritual Care and Bereavement services in the NHS. She understood her role to be that of helping others to 'make music with what remains': frail, elderly people reaching end of life; grieving partners embarking on a new life alone; people of any age receiving devastating news. As for Perlman, often it is those who have had to cope with setbacks in life who are most sanguine in the face of disaster; they see the three good strings and not the single, broken one.

It may take us years to find the good strings. After a major bereavement, we may need to focus on the silent, empty space left by the 'broken string', and mourn its loss, before we can begin to think about 'what remains'. But the common experience of grieving people is to find, eventually, that there is music still to be played.

As I listen to grieving people, I often hear the stirrings of transformation. Some no longer fear death. Some are surprised at their resilience. Some, as we have seen, discover a new empathy for those who suffer. Some find their value-system changed. Wertheimer, in her study of people bereaved by suicide (as she herself was), found that material things had become less important for some, and what mattered more was valuing people, and attending to the quality of life. For some family members, the suicide brought them closer as they sought to bring something positive out of the tragedy. Some changed career, often entering one of the helping professions. Some found themselves asking profound questions of their lives that they would never have thought to ask before the death.

Parkes uses a healing analogy: 'Just as broken bones may end up stronger than unbroken ones, so the experience of grieving can strengthen and bring maturity to those who have previously been protected from misfortune.'[36] 'My life is lived with a different intensity,' Cave noted, after the death of his son. 'Not the burning intensity of youth, but something else – a kind of spiritual audacity. I've noticed this in a lot of grieving people ... a kind of zeal.'[37] Francis Weller has led people in communal grief rituals for many years. 'There is some strange intimacy between grief and aliveness,' he writes, 'some sacred exchange between what seems unbearable and what is most exquisitely alive.'[38]

Begin where you are

It's important to acknowledge that everyone grieves differently. No two losses are the same. There is no timetable to bereavement and no short cut through it. On the whole, those who are bereaved do not have the benefit of hindsight; for some, it can feel as if the pain will never end.

Reassurance rarely works in therapy and is generally to be avoided. On occasion, however, I may say to a bereaved person, 'It feels just now as if the pain will never end. I wonder if it is hard for you to imagine a time when it will feel easier and you will find new purpose for your life.' Often, people recently bereaved can't imagine anything like 'moving on'; but the mere possibility of the pain lessening can be a source of hope.

For some reading this, then, talk of a 'spirituality of grief' will sound hollow or fanciful. Your grief may be so overwhelming that it will be impossible to imagine it connecting you more holistically to yourself, to others or to the transcendent. You may not experience any new insights, only fog; and talk of personal growth, or heeding a call to 'make music with what remains', may only add to your burden.

Spirituality begins, as I've said, with accepting 'what is': acknowledging the world the way we find it. You may discover yourself sitting, like the biblical figure of Job, on the ash heap, reeling from recent events. It may be that your grief seems to lack any redemptive possibilities. If that is where you are, it can help simply to acknowledge it and resist imagining that you ought to feel any different. This may not be the time for the language of hope; indeed, it may be the language of lament that speaks for you, such as that found in the ancient poetry of Psalm 88. But what I hesitate to say to my clients, I gently say here: it won't always feel this way; grief moves on.

Grief moves on. And the voice of grief whispers: all is not loss.

Notes

1 Dovid Diamand, 2019, *Making Music With What Remains*, published independently, https://www.amazon.com/Making-Music-Remains-Dovid-Diamand/dp/1795070587, accessed 08.05.2025.

2 E. Kübler-Ross, 1970, *On Death and Dying*, London: Tavistock Publications. The idea that there are discrete 'stages of grief' was popularized by the psychiatrist Elisabeth Kübler-Ross in the late 1960s. Her theory applied to the grief experienced by the terminally ill people with whom she was conducting her research. To be fair to her research, her 'stages' were never intended to apply to the bereaved, so perhaps we should not be surprised if bereaved people don't recognize their experience in her 'stages' model.

3 C. Lloyd, 2023, *You Are Not Alone*, London: Bloomsbury Tonic, pp. 6–7.

4 J. Didion, 2005, *The Year of Magical Thinking*, New York, NY: A. A. Knopf, pp. 26–7.

5 American Psychiatric Association, 2022, *Diagnostic and Statistical Manual of Mental Disorders, Fifth Edition, Text Revision*, Washington, DC: American Psychiatric Association.

6 I. D. Yalom and M. Yalom, 2021, *A Matter of Death and Life*, London: Piatkus, p. 175.

7 N. Cave and S. O'Hagan, 2023, *Faith, Hope and Carnage*, Edinburgh: Canongate Books, p. 42.

8 Cave and O'Hagan, *Faith*, p. 169.

9 C. M. Parkes, 1972, *Bereavement: Studies of grief in adult life*, New York, NY: International Universities Press, p. 5.

10 A. Wertheimer, 1991, *A Special Scar*, London: Routledge, p. 214.

11 Cave and O'Hagan, *Faith*, p. 220.

BEREAVEMENT

12 F. Weller, 2015, *The Wild Edge of Sorrow: Rituals of renewal and the sacred work of grief*, Berkeley, CA: North Atlantic Books, p. 1.

13 Yalom and Yalom, *Matter of Death*, p. 161.

14 Cave and O'Hagan, *Faith*, p. 168; emphasis added.

15 J. Humphrys, 2010, *The Welcome Visitor*, London: Hodder & Stoughton, p. 266.

16 S. Freud, 1984, 'Mourning and Melancholia', trans. J. Strachey, in A. Richards (ed.), *On Metapsychology: The theory of psychoanalysis*, Harmondsworth: Pelican, pp. 251–68.

17 Parkes, *Bereavement*, p. 83.

18 J. Samuel, 2017, *Grief Works*, London: Penguin, p. 224.

19 Parkes, *Bereavement*, p. 8.

20 C. S. Lewis, 1966, *A Grief Observed*, London: Faber & Faber, p. 12.

21 J. Bowlby, 1991, *Loss: Sadness and depression*, London: Penguin, p. 442.

22 'Object relations' theory uses the term 'object' to describe our internalized versions of significant people in our lives. I prefer the phrase 'inner presence' to describe, in more personal terms, a person we have admitted to our internal worlds. Their inner presence does not vanish when they die. Mourning is the process of learning to decouple the inner presence from the loved one it represents in the external world; of relinquishing the attempt to locate our loved ones 'out there'; and of finding a new space within us, where we can relate to them with less pain.

23 J. W. Worden, 1991, *Grief Counselling and Grief Therapy: A handbook for the mental health practitioner*, 2nd ed., London: Routledge, p. 18.

24 For those interested in exploring models of grief in more depth, the pictures I have given here each relate to a different theory. The see-saw represents Stroebe and Schut's (1999) dual process model. The doughnut illustrates Tonkin's (1996) model of 'growing around grief'. The task-list relates to Worden's (1982) model of the four 'tasks' of grieving. The image of a journey illustrates Bowlby and Parkes's four 'phases' of mourning. The invisible thread pictures Silverman and Klass's (1996) notion of 'continuing bonds', explored in a book of that title. I have not included Kübler-Ross's well-known five-stage model here, as it applies to terminal patients and not the bereaved.

25 Worden, *Grief Counselling*, p. 16.

26 Parkes, *Bereavement*, p. 6.

27 The notion of 'continuing bonds' has become an important aspect of grief theory, in contrast to Freud's view that successful grieving involves withdrawing connection from the deceased. See D. Klass, P. R. Silverman and S. L. Nickman, 1996, *Continuing Bonds: New understandings of grief*, Washington, DC: Taylor & Francis.

28 Lewis, *Grief Observed*, p. 42.
29 Cave and O'Hagan, *Faith*, p. 106.
30 Wertheimer, *Special Scar*, p. 187.
31 R. D. Romanyshyn, 1999, *The Soul in Grief: Love, death and transformation*, Berkeley, CA: North Atlantic Books, p. 151.
32 S. Freud, 1943, *The Future of an Illusion*, trans. W. D. Robson-Scott, London: Hogarth Press, p. 33.
33 Yalom and Yalom, *Matter of Death*, p. 221.
34 Didion, *Year of Magical Thinking*, p. 150.
35 Cave and O'Hagan, *Faith*, p. 31.
36 Parkes, *Bereavement*, p. 5.
37 Cave and O'Hagan, *Faith*, p. 159.
38 Weller, *Wild Edge*, p. 1.

2

Mortality

What is your life? For you are a mist that appears for a little while and then vanishes. (James 4.14, NRSV)

In the early days of the Internet, I stumbled across a computer app that fascinated me. It was a 'death clock' widget: a small counter you could place on your computer screen to watch the days and hours, minutes and seconds count down to the moment of your death. It was very crude: it based your life expectancy on a few criteria, including your current age, sex, and whether you smoked and took regular exercise. But it worked as a reminder that life is finite and precious; for a while, it hung cheerfully at the top right-hand corner of my screen, updating my allotted span every second. I forget when it was that I was due to die.

There are many versions of this clock available online today and, of course, none can really give us a date with any accuracy. But I remain intrigued by the idea of such a reminder. In the past, perhaps before the advent of modern hospitals, human mortality was more within sight. Deaths largely took place in the home and most communities would have had all-too-frequent reminders of death in their midst. For centuries, worshippers hearing Psalm 90 were exhorted to pray: 'teach us to number our days, that we may apply our hearts unto wisdom' (Ps. 90.12, AV). Older graveyards are full of images and symbols, often carved on seventeenth-century tombstones, reminding us to keep our mortality before our eyes: skulls, bones, skeletons, candles, hourglasses.

Nowadays, we have fewer reminders and the voices exhorting us to number our days have been stilled. Like our ancestors, most of us, I suspect, would rather not think about our mortality. The sixteenth-century philosopher, Michel de Montaigne, observed the human tendency to keep pushing our death beyond the foreseeable future: 'Neither is any man so old and decrepit, who ... does not think he has yet twenty good years to come.'[1] Two hundred years later, Francois de la Rochefoucauld wrote his famous maxim: 'Neither the sun nor death can be looked at without winking.'[2] Freud thought it impossible to stare at the sun, asserting that 'at bottom, no one believes in his own death', and that 'in the unconscious every one of us is convinced of his own immortality'.[3] In a powerful thought experiment, C. S. Lewis suggested that we cannot look at our hands and believe that one day they will belong to mere skeletons. I tried this once, standing at Lewis's grave in Headington Quarry, near Oxford. It was easy enough to believe that Lewis's hands lay six feet below as the hands of a skeleton; but to look at my own hand and imagine? I found myself winking.

In this chapter, I want to think about our mortality as a form of loss: something Irvin Yalom calls the 'wound of mortality'. This wound, this loss, is painful, and we try to avoid it. Montaigne notes that we defend ourselves from the fact of our death by kicking it over the horizon and convincing ourselves that we don't have to think about it *yet*. Perhaps if we can keep it out of sight, we can maintain a belief that we will live for ever. The realization of our mortality punctures this illusion. It wrecks our belief that we have infinite choices, and all the time in the world to achieve our dreams or mend our relationships. Often, we leave it too late. Time and again, I hear people tell me that they had no idea how quickly the years would speed past or how soon a family member would die.

The wound of mortality asks to be grieved. Somehow, we must come to terms with our shrinking options, crumbling dreams and ageing bodies, and with the fear of death itself. Yet, as we have been exploring throughout this book, I want to look at the possibility that, in the face of our mortality, 'all is not loss'. The psalmist urged us to number our days, *'that we may apply our hearts to wisdom'*. There is deep wisdom in keeping the fact of our death in mind.

In what follows, I will look at what can happen when we ignore the truth of our mortality and avoid the work of grieving its wound. I will consider some ways in which our mortal selves have been paid more attention in the past and explore the possibility that such a recognition of our mortality can be a doorway to spiritual transformation.

Death denial

Death is a hard topic for small talk. Despite some valiant attempts to provide contexts in which death can be more easily spoken about,[4] we mostly avoid the subject. It is hard to speak about death without evoking the thought of our own mortality. This can leave us feeling anxious: de la Rochefoucauld's maxim implies we can no more look death in the face than we can stare at the sun. Instead, we typically bury our death anxiety: in the language of psychotherapy, we *repress* it, forcing it out of our awareness and into the realm of the unconscious. However, it takes considerable energy to keep the lid on our unconscious, like trying to hold a football under water. Our death anxiety has a way of popping up and influencing how we feel and behave. Freud thought that this unconscious material could be detected as it leaked out in dreams, jokes and slips of the tongue, or was evidenced in acts of forgetting, making mistakes or self-sabotage. Sometimes these minor eruptions are merely amusing. I have witnessed plenty of dark humour in the funeral industry, for example. At other times, our death anxiety can send a wrecking-ball through our settled lives.

Death denial often appears in the language we use. We often avoid the words 'death' or 'died' and say that someone has 'passed', 'gone', 'departed', 'been taken' or 'deceased'. We use phrases such as 'when my time comes', 'kick the bucket' and 'meet my maker'. Perhaps we have a superstitious fear that if we name death, it will come to find us.

Our anxiety about death will surface differently at various stages of life. It is not unusual for small children to be curious about death as they experience autumn, or the death of a pet or a close relative. Adults may rush to reassure, or silence, a small child and thereby give him or her a first lesson in death avoidance. Later, themes of death may come to the fore again in adolescence: for example, in the exploration of 'gothic' styles, in horror films, in violent gaming or in risk-taking behaviours.

But it is typically not until mid life that anxiety about our mortality begins to bite. Mid life involves the task of negotiating a new relationship with death. We become more aware of our regrets, the shrinking of our options, our ageing bodies, the limits of our potential, our fading dreams, and of the vista laid out before us as we come 'over the hill' and begin the descent.

As we grow older, if we are unable to befriend our mortality, but only repress it further, our death anxiety is liable to cause behaviours that may amount to a 'mid-life crisis'. Some may end a decades-long relationship and attempt to 'start again', with another partner and a new family. Others may use sex as a defence against the prospect of death. After the death of his wife, Irvin Yalom found he was invaded by powerful and persistent sexual thoughts. 'I am flooded with both desire and shame. I wince at such disloyalty to Marilyn, buried only weeks ago.'[5] He argues that throwing ourselves into life-giving intimacy and generative potency is a means of screening off our death anxiety. For still others, anxiety may issue in a fervent attempt to stay looking young, through gym regimes or cosmetic surgery. None of these behaviours is necessarily self-defeating, but neither do they help us come to terms with the wound of mortality.

There are many moments in life that have the potential to put us in touch with our mortality, if we are willing to listen. Such 'awakening experiences', as Yalom describes them,[6] often occur at times of tragedy or during normal transitions in the life course. They almost always involve loss. It may be the empty nest or the menopause that underlines that our phase of generativity and close family life is over. It may be the death of a parent, which quietly whispers that we're next in line. It may be redundancy or being overlooked for promotion, which caps our ambitions and reinforces our limitations. Even those who are financially successful may wonder at the value of a bonus that will not cure all ills or buy them a longer life. Retirement may be another trigger. It is often held up as the promise of a golden future, away from the daily grind; yet I have often noticed how colleagues approaching retirement have prevaricated and delayed, staying at work an extra year or two. When retirement approaches, it is understandable if we hesitate to leave the world of paid employment, to embark on a new and perhaps final chapter.

These moments will come, one way or another. We can flee from them or accept them as an invitation to befriend our mortality, to tend its 'wound'. Only by grieving the losses of our finitude can we discover its transforming potential.

Memento mori

Ours has not always been a death-denying culture. From the dawn of written records, across many cultures and religious traditions, we encounter the exhortation to *remember death* – the so-called memento mori, which literally means 'remember [that you are] to die'.

Death's apologists have been many: the ancient Greek philosopher Democritus hung out in cemeteries; Montaigne advocated placing a writing desk to have a good view of a graveyard, to help concentrate the mind. Socrates claimed that 'the true philosophers are always occupied in the practice of dying'. The Stoics took the view that to live well we must learn to die well. Cicero believed that the study of philosophy was nothing but a preparation for death. St Benedict said one must 'keep death daily before one's eyes'. Medieval monks reputedly each kept a human skull by their beds. Montaigne tells us that, in Ancient Egypt, the host of a banquet, 'in the height of [the] feasting and mirth, caused a dried skeleton of a man to be brought into the room to serve for a memento to [the] guests'.[7] We can only imagine how the atmosphere changed.

Today, such reminders of our mortality are rare. But, from the late medieval period in Europe, death was represented visually in a range of contexts, particularly in the wake of the Black Death. The memento mori was symbolized in many ways: the carved rotting corpse of the *transi* ('cadaver tomb'); images of a fading flower, a guttering candle, a skull or an hourglass painted on canvas or carved on a tombstone; the *danse macabre*, in which rich and poor alike are depicted as being led away by cheerful skeletons; and the device of the 'three living and the three dead' found in manuscripts and painted on church walls.

Sometimes these images were accompanied by words. This is a typical example:

My glass is run
And yours is running
Be wise in time
Your day is coming
(Chidiock Tichborne, 1562–86, 'Elegy')[8]

This seems intended to bring home the inevitability of death. Others emphasize the fleeting impermanence of this life compared to the reality of the world to come. At Dunkeld Cathedral, the impressive Atholl Monument in the Chapter House proclaims, in Latin:

We are dust and shadow
Death is the door to life

Nowadays, we tend to shrink from such reminders of our mortality. Perhaps we enjoy brief flirtations with all things ghoulish at Hallowe'en or participate in Mexican-style Day of the Dead celebrations. These festivals originated in the remembrance of ancestors, martyrs or the 'faithful departed'; currently, they seem more to do with providing a brief moment to let death out of the closet. In a culture of pervasive death denial, perhaps we still have a need to take a safe peek at our mortality. Some attempts to engage with it are more deliberate: Death Cafes, for example, legitimize talking about death and dying; there are men's groups that explore life transitions by digging graves and lying in them;[9] and the death clock apps keep ticking. But these are the exceptions.

On the whole, we try not to 'stare at the sun'. We cloak death with discreet euphemisms. At best we have a faint intuition, or cultural memory, that there is benefit in remembering our mortality.

But what if we were to keep our mortality always in mind and learn to 'number our days'? Jung advised us 'to discover in death a goal towards which one can strive', suggesting that if we shrink from this it will rob the second half of life of its purpose.[10] For the Buddha, it was an encounter with old age, sickness and finally a corpse that helped him to see the transience of life; he was inspired to leave the comfort of his palace and seek a life as a homeless mendicant. It seems to be the wisdom of the ages that contemplating death, especially our own deaths, can be transformative. Irvin Yalom sums up the purpose of the memento mori tradition in an elegant formula: 'Although the physicality of death destroys us, the idea of death saves us.'[11]

It is only by grieving the wound of our mortality that we can encounter its transforming potential.

Mortality and spiritual transformation

How might the idea of death save us? What spirituality might we derive from the memento mori tradition for today? We turn to consider the possibility that the idea of death can transform the quality of our lives in the present.

Accepting impermanence

One way this can work is by contemplating the transience of life. In Buddhist thought, one of the marks of material things is *anicca*: 'impermanence'. Our compulsive attempt to grasp or possess the ephemeral things of this world will only add to our suffering. Freud believed that by being aware of the impermanence of all things, we will value them more. Yalom insists that the 'way to value life ... is to be aware that these experiences are destined to be lost'.[12] We can appreciate the beauty of a flower at the height of its glory all the more by knowing that in a few weeks it will have withered. Its very impermanence invites us to savour the moment: 'everything is a gift, and nothing lasts'.[13]

Human lives are filled with such moments. We can look back at an old photograph and remember a loved one with fondness: but what if, when the photo was taken, we could keep in mind that one day that scene will be irrecoverable, gone for ever? How much more might we cherish it? This thought does not need be morose, if we treat every click of the shutter as a simple invitation to pause, notice and savour. We can practice the same appreciation when alone. Even the dullest day can seem precious when we stop and take it in. As Bob Whorton, a hospice chaplain, observed, 'We realise the value of a normal day when it has gone. Then we may long to be bored again by the humdrum ordinary life we have lived.'[14]

Awareness of the impermanence of our lives can also lead us to reorder our values. Atul Gawande describes how a near-fatal road accident caused Lisa Carstensen to change direction and end up as a Stanford professor who studied ageing. She noticed that as people got older, they became better at appreciating life. Just as her brush with death had changed her perspective, she surmised that 'how we seek to spend our time may depend on how much time we perceive ourselves to have'.[15] She found that people who think they have a shorter time left to live prioritized close relationships and everyday pleasures over the novelty of seeking new people, information and achievements.

Another response to impermanence is gratitude. Simon Boas,

knowing that he had just months to live, wrote that to be alive today is similar to winning the lottery: 'Our glasses are half full, or perhaps even fuller, and, when we remember this, we should be filled with exuberance and gratitude.'[16] His only regret is that he did not discover how to practice this attitude to life until death came knocking at his door.

Working through anxieties

One objection to keeping our death always before our eyes is that this sounds like a recipe for living in a state of almost permanent anxiety. We cannot, as we have seen, stare at the sun. As we have seen, death anxiety can lurk just beneath the surface and appear in strange guises. While working with people who are bereaved or dying, I am not immune. I hear so many stories. It's easy to imagine that every abdominal pain I experience is the beginning of *my* cancer story. Death comes to me in dreams: a Victorian chimneysweep forces his way into my house; I have to choose from a drawer-full of black socks; an enemy force attacks my castle.

How, then, can we follow the advice, memento mori, and not live anxious lives? In part, the answer to this depends on what it is we fear about death in the first place. For some, it is the thought of being dead that scares them. This may take the form of uncertainty about an afterlife and what it might be like. Some fear the vulnerability of being unable to protect their bodies after death. They may recoil from the thought of being buried in a lonely place or resting in the dark. Some are fearful of 'nothingness'. Julian Barnes gave his meditation on mortality a deliberately ambiguous title that neatly captures this dichotomy: *Nothing to Be Frightened of.*[17] Although such fears may seem quite irrational, they are felt as real.

Other fears have more basis in reality: the possibility of being in pain at the end of life, say, or fears about how loved ones will cope after we have died. It may be helpful to voice our fears about the process of dying to a palliative care specialist. While they cannot predict the precise course of our death, they can often dispel myths and reassure us with information about the process of dying and the palliative care available. Likewise, taking the opportunity to speak to a skilled listener can help us to work through our anxieties and sadness about leaving our loved ones. It can also help to support us as we adjust to a final illness.

If we do not believe that the soul has any ongoing life after death, we may more easily be able to think our way out of death anxiety. The Greek philosopher Epicurus argued that, since we will not be there to experience the fact of our death, being dead cannot harm us. We will return to a state of non-existence, not unlike the situation before we were born. Such clear logic will work for some; but for others, it will not touch the 'irrational' fear that lies buried in the unconscious. One way or another, as Nick Cave notes, 'You learn to make peace with the idea of death as best you can.'[18]

For those who believe in an afterlife, death anxiety may be still more complex. Some may find the notion of an afterlife a comfort. For others, addressing this fear may require the working through of inherited folktales and medieval depictions of heaven and hell or the idea of confinement to a half-life in an underworld somewhere. Perhaps the mystical tradition can offer some reassurance here, with its deep conviction that love lies at the heart of the universe, and that, in the words of Mother Julian, 'All will be well, and all will be well, and all manner of thing will be well.'[19]

Befriending our death

Another approach to death anxiety is the idea of befriending our death. We have thought about mortality as a wound that needs to heal or a loss that needs to be grieved. The wound is the knowledge that our bodies are ageing and will one day die. In coming to terms with this fact, we lose the comforting illusion that we can live for ever or that death is a mere theoretical possibility, somewhere over the rainbow. Befriending our death involves coming to accept that death is a part of life: it is normal, universal and, we might even say, 'good'. Befriending death involves demystifying what may seem uncanny. 'Let us disarm him of his novelty and strangeness,' wrote Montaigne, 'let us converse and be familiar with him, and have nothing so frequent in our thoughts as death.'[20]

Treating death as a part of life, and not as a robber or intruder, can help us to come to terms with it and feel that, in most circumstances, death could be natural – 'OK', even. When the Olympic cyclist Chris Hoy announced publicly that his cancer was terminal, he told the *Sunday Times*: 'As unnatural as it feels, this is nature.'[21] Accepting that death is a part of life – a familiar friend rather than a grim reaper or an apocalyptic horseman – can allow us to be more sanguine about it.

Some learn to accept this from an early age. Brian Thorne tells of a mystical experience he had as a child, one Good Friday, in which an overwhelming experience of 'uncontrollable grief' gave way to a sense that 'life and death are not in opposition but belong to a greater unity'.[22] For others, befriending death comes as a resolution to the mid-life crisis. In my early 40s, I found myself turning to the stories and novels of the Orkney writer George Mackay Brown as I wrestled with my own finitude. Although GMB hardly left the Orkney Isles in his lifetime, he imparted to me a universal sense that death belongs to life and, moreover, could be *good*. The great wheel of human life has turned in Orkney for upwards of eight millennia. My ancestors are buried there in the sand. The thought that one day I might join them and take up my place in the noble procession of lives and deaths feels wholesome and good.

I hesitate to say this, as the experience of the dying is sometimes a very long way from being 'good'. Yet even here, on the occasions I have dared to wonder aloud to a person with an incurable illness whether their death could somehow be OK, I have never been met with disagreement. And although a dying person might understandably feel unlucky to have contracted this or that rare cancer, there is comfort in knowing that death itself is a universal experience that belongs to the whole of humanity. We're in this together, as Simon Boas is happy to remind us in the closing words his death-bed book: he wishes us well 'when [our] turn comes'.[23]

Keeping the end in view

If we can normalize death, it becomes easier to keep our end in view; to recognize, in the graveside words of the Anglican service of burial: 'In the midst of life we are in death.'[24]

'Keep the end in view' is simply another way of saying, 'Memento mori.' It needn't be full of skulls and crossbones. Ian Bradley observes that, in West Highland tradition, it was one of the first duties of a newly married wife to sew a shroud for her husband: an acknowledgement at the very beginning of married life that one day it would come to an end.[25]

At my allotment, I notice plants growing, fruiting and dying. I watch the seasons roll around: the lush summer growth yellowing and shrivelling under winter's cleansing scourge. Death is an annual event. Each year is another year; life moves on. It reminds me that my days are numbered; I have only so many seasons on this earth. Inside my shed, I have pinned a quote from Montaigne: 'then let death take me planting my cabbages, indifferent to him, and still less of my gardens not being finished.'[26]

Death is part of life. We didn't agree to this in advance but only learned of it after being born into this world. One of our tasks here is to 'sign the deal' of being human. This means accepting the gift of life on the basis that, one day, we will need to give it back: we are leaseholders, not freeholders. Our task is to grieve the wound of this discovery; to accept that 'in the midst of life we are in death'.

Befriending our death means that we no longer need to see life as a desperate bucket-list of 101 things to do before we die, but as a gift of days to be lived out in gratitude. 'Keeping the end in view' might mean we adopt certain practices that help us to do so. Writing a will is one way we explicitly acknowledge that one day we will die: this is not an easy admission and, unsurprisingly, less than half of UK adults have made one.[27] Decluttering may be another, with its tacit meaning of detaching from material things and preparing to travel light. Seeking to live more simply and sustainably is also a way of recognizing that our finite time on this earth is just one lifespan among many. In the Christian tradition, on Ash Wednesday, worshippers receive the sign of the cross on the forehead in ash, while hearing these words: 'Remember that you are dust, and to dust you shall return.' In Buddhism, there is a tradition of meditation on the nine stages of a decaying corpse. Nowadays, we may not wish to sit before a body in the open air as nature in all its forms consumes it. But a walk through a graveyard or a visit to a historic burial site can make death seem more familiar. The month before he died, Simon Boas wrote, 'I have found that talking about death, preparing for it and accepting it, have helped me enjoy life all the more, to prioritise the important things over the trivial, and to feel a little more compassion for other people.'[28] He had discovered the wisdom of his forerunner Montaigne: 'He who should teach men to die would at the same time teach them to live.'[29]

Legacy

One further way in which we might tend the wound of our mortality is to reflect on the legacy that we will leave behind when we die. True, death is the end of us in this world; but our influence will continue for some time to come in the hearts and memories of those we leave behind. Recently, I attended the funeral of a distinguished Palestinian doctor. In the funeral address, his son quoted an Arabic proverb that translates as 'What's left is in your life now.' This neatly captures a sense of the ongoing presence of the person in the lives of those who knew him. Another funeral address recalled a similar phrase: 'Look for her among her friends.'[30] This underlines the truth that no man is an island but we exist as beings-in-community:

others are alive in us as an inner presence, and they remain within long after the physical person has died. Yalom uses the metaphor of 'rippling' to describe the ways in which our influence will live on, even after we have slipped out of sight, like a stone dropped into water. Ripples do not go on for ever; eventually, all of us will be forgotten.[31] But the prospect remains that our influence may live on for generations to come. This thought may spur us to leave a legacy, whether in writing, in the creation of an artefact, in an act of kindness or even as a financial endowment. In this way, too, the contemplation of our mortality may enrich our lives in the present.

The wound of our mortality, like any loss, asks to be grieved. As we come to terms with it, we may discover a surprising truth: far from being gloomy and morbid, *remembering death enhances life.*

Notes

1 M. de Montaigne, 1877, 'That to Study Philosophy Is to Learn to Die', trans. C. Cotton, in W. Carew Hazlitt, ed., *Essays of Michel de Montaigne*, London: Reeves and Turner, at https://www.gutenberg.org/ebooks/3600, accessed 14.04.2025.

2 F. de la Rochefoucauld, 1871, *Reflections; or Sentences and Moral Maxims*, trans. J. W. Willis Bund and J. H. Friswell, London: Simpson Low, Son, and Marston, Project Gutenberg (release date Oct. 2005; updated 25 Jan. 2013), at https://www.gutenberg.org/files/9105/9105-h/9105-h.htm, accessed 14.04.2025.

3 S. Freud, 1985, 'Our Attitude Towards Death', trans. J. Strachey, in A. Dickson (ed.), *Civilization, Society and Religion: Group psychology, civilization and its discontents and other works*, London: Pelican, p. 77.

4 The Death Cafe social franchise is one example; see https://deathcafe.com.

5 I. D. Yalom and M. Yalom, 2021, *A Matter of Death and Life*, London: Piatkus, pp. 169–70.

6 I. D. Yalom, 2008, *Staring at the Sun: Being at peace with your own mortality*, London: Piatkus, p. 31.

7 de Montaigne, 'That to Study Philosophy Is to Learn to Die', at https://www.gutenberg.org/ebooks/3600, accessed 14.04.2025.

8 Chidiock Tichborne (1562–86), 'Elegy', cited in I. Bradley, 2022, *The Coffin Roads*, Edinburgh: Birlinn Ltd, p. 92.

9 For example, see F. Weller, 2015, *The Wild Edge of Sorrow: Rituals*

of renewal and the sacred work of grief, Berkeley, CA: North Atlantic Books, p. 134.

10 C. G. Jung, 1975, Structure and Dynamics of the Psyche: The collected works of C. G. Jung, vol. 8, trans. R. F. C. Hull, Princeton: Princeton University Press, p. 520, at https://jungiancenter.org/wp-content/uploads/2023/09/vol-8-the-structure-and-dynamics-of-the-psyche.pdf, accessed 14.04.2025.

11 Yalom, *Staring at the Sun*, p. 33.

12 Yalom, *Staring at the Sun*, p. 147.

13 Weller, *Wild Edge*, p. 24.

14 B. Whorton, 2015, *Voices from the Hospice*, London: SCM Press, p. 29.

15 Atul Gawande, 2015, *Being Mortal: Illness, medicine, and what matters in the end*, London: Wellcome Collection, p. 97.

16 S. Boas, 2024, *A Beginner's Guide to Dying*, London: Swift Press, p. 50.

17 J. Barnes, 2008, *Nothing to be Frightened of*, London: Jonathan Cape.

18 N. Cave and S. O'Hagan, 2023, *Faith, Hope and Carnage*, Edinburgh: Canongate Books, p. 199.

19 Julian of Norwich, 1987, *Revelations of Divine Love*, London: Hodder & Stoughton, p. 55.

20 de Montaigne, 'That to Study Philosophy Is to Learn to Die', at https://www.gutenberg.org/ebooks/3600, accessed 14.04.2025.

21 A. Lamche and A. Boyd, 2024, 'Cyclist Chris Hoy Announces That His Cancer Is Terminal', *BBC News*, 19 October, at https://www.bbc.co.uk/news/articles/cj4dr9xdxgro, accessed 14.04.2025.

22 B. Thorne, 1998, *Person-Centred Counselling and Christian Spirituality*, London: Whurr Publishers Ltd, p. 92.

23 Boas, *Beginner's Guide*, p. 138.

24 Church of England, 1981, The Book of Common Prayer, Cambridge: Cambridge University Press, p. 332.

25 Bradley, *Coffin Roads*, p. 12.

26 de Montaigne, 'That to Study Philosophy Is to Learn to Die', at https://www.gutenberg.org/ebooks/3600, accessed 14.04.2025.

27 The National Will Register, 2023, 'Two-fifths of UK adults not discussed instructions after death, new wills report finds', at https://www.nationalwillregister.co.uk/news/two-fifths-of-uk-adults-not-discussed-instructions-after-death-new-wills-report-finds, accessed 14.04.2025.

28 Boas, *Beginner's Guide*, pp. 5–6.

29 de Montaigne, 'That to Study Philosophy Is to Learn to Die', at https://www.gutenberg.org/ebooks/3600, accessed 14.04.2025.

30 Yalom, *Staring at the Sun*, p. 85.

31 Yalom, *Staring at the Sun*, p. 83f.

3

Dependence

> Even though our outer nature is wasting away, our inner nature is being renewed day by day. (2 Cor. 4.16, NRSV)

Loss is an inevitable part of being human. All of us will, sooner or later, experience significant loss of a magnitude that will trigger disabling grief: a break-up, a regret, a failure, a death. Yet there is another kind of loss that is even more ubiquitous. Unless we die young, it will come to us all. This kind of loss is the steady diminishment that occurs across the human life course: progressive disability, illness, ageing and dying. On the face of it, such universal losses indicate that life is a one-way street, and diminishment is only to be feared. In this chapter, I explore whether such pessimism is justified and consider again the possibility that 'all is not loss'.

We don't want to think about enduring and progressive disability, the ignominies of ageing, the possibility of serious illness or, indeed, the process of dying. All of these raise the spectre of a fearful state that many of us spend a lifetime trying to prevent, that of *dependence*. Many who say they don't fear death itself will be less sanguine about disability and increasing dependence, with the shrinking of choice and autonomy that this implies. As Dr Margaret McCartney observes, 'It's clear to me that old and very old people seldom fear death itself, but fear being alone, or in pain, or becoming dependent on others.'[1] Christie Watson, a former nurse, is blunter: 'Dying is not always the worst thing. Living a long life and suffering cruelty in old age is the terrible fate that waits for many of us.'[2]

Becoming dependent is a form of loss. 'It is not death that the very old tell me they fear,' writes Atul Gawande. 'It is what happens short of death – losing their hearing, their memory, their best friends, their way of life.'³ The losses associated with increasing dependence evoke a slow-burning grief or what Susan Roos has termed 'chronic sorrow'.⁴ However, it is not always obvious quite what is being grieved. Grieving our loss of 'independence' is an umbrella term for a multitude of losses. In this chapter, we will consider those that stem from progressive disability, ageing, illness and dying.

Progressive disability

I don't remember the exact occasion. I recall standing in a side aisle of a packed cathedral in Edinburgh, surrounded by family. My son was singing in the choir. My father was standing in the row behind. My mother was sitting next to him in a wheelchair at the end of the row.

I do remember the hymn we were singing. It was Charlotte Elliott's 'Just as I am' (1835), sung to the tune 'Saffron Walden'. We sang the fourth verse:

> Just as I am, poor, wretched, blind!
> Sight, riches, healing of the mind
> all that I need, in you to find:
> O Lamb of God, I come.

In a momentary breath between verses, in the murmured hush of the great cathedral, I heard a howl go up behind me. It sounded like the anguish of a wounded animal or the unearthly cry of an exiled spirit. I turned my head to look for the source of the noise. There sat my mother in her wheelchair, wearing a tortured expression. She had been diagnosed with motor neurone disease a year before. The condition can not only affect the body's physical control but also make the sufferer more emotionally volatile. I realized the hymn had touched her. The thought that she could come to the 'Lamb of God' – *just as I am* – seemed to have provoked this great cry.

The hymn was written by Charlotte Elliott and first published in the second edition of *The Invalid's Hymn Book* of 1841, of which Elliott later became editor.[5] Elliott was no stranger to disability. In her early 30s, she found herself battling fatigue, which we might nowadays diagnose as chronic fatigue (syndrome), or a post-viral condition. She described herself in a relentless fight against 'bodily feelings of almost overpowering weakness and languor and exhaustion'.[6] Perhaps something of her overcoming spirit was woven into these verses. She knew what it meant to feel helpless and dependent. She knew what it meant to be accepted by God, 'just as I am'. And through her hymn, across the decades, her liberating insight touched my mother. In this chapter, we will think more about the grief of progressive disability and whether there can be any more to this than loss.

Ageing

'We accumulate the years,' wrote Stewart Henderson, whose words are set to music by folk singer Yvonne Lyon in a song of that title.[7] I find it a haunting and evocative phrase that speaks of the inevitability of ageing. I imagine the years, like the silent accumulation of layers of snow, piling up on us. Perhaps it is not until we look back at old photos of events, the memories of which still feel fresh, that we realize the magnitude of this accumulation. Google Photos serves up reminders on my phone of events that happened 'on this day' 10 or 15 years ago. As I look, I'm staggered that a memorable family holiday is now 10 years in the past; or that it's 15 years since I left that job.

As we accumulate the years, our bodies age. They, too, remind us of the passage of time, the inevitability of ageing and the likelihood of increasing infirmity and diminishment. Irvin Yalom writes of his experience when, in his mid 40s, his optician examined him and declared that his presbyopia was right on cue. Yalom protested: surely, *he* didn't need reading glasses? Surely, the changes of ageing are what happen to

DEPENDENCE

other people? Yet our bodies say otherwise. And as we become increasingly attuned to the process of ageing, we are also confronted with the inevitability of our own death. Physical ageing is not just a series of mild inconveniences, but an awakening to the existential fact that we are heading down a one-way street named Mortality.

Each step of the ageing process represents a loss. As I sat in the physiotherapist's waiting room, nursing a sore knee, I caught sight of a poster that cheerfully proclaimed I lose eight percent of my muscle mass every decade. I tried to do the maths. If I had 100 per cent of my muscle at the age of 20, how much did I have left when I was 50? What would I have left at 60, 70 or 80? If I lived to be 100, would I have any muscles left?

And it's not only about muscle loss: we can look forward to decreased bone density, worsening sight and hearing, and hormonal changes. Our skin will wrinkle, and our hair will become thinner and greyer. We will lose beauty and suppleness. Chronic health conditions are not unlikely: arthritis, diabetes and cardiovascular disease, to name a few. Our memory may deteriorate and our thinking slow. Or worse. For many of us, ageing will diminish our capabilities to the point where we become dependent on others for our basic needs.

How do we grieve these losses? Or *do* we grieve them? Perhaps because ageing is universal, we don't see it as a loss; or we spend so much effort trying to look and stay young that we cannot bear to look ageing full in the face. Montaigne reflected that the death of our youthfulness is 'a harder death than the final dissolution of a languishing body'.[8] Yet, by avoiding the fact of our ageing, we may overlook the reality that, with ageing, 'all is not loss': there may be a spirituality to ageing that is there for us if we remain open to it.

Illness

A different kind of dependence is forced upon us when we are ill. It is no coincidence that the word 'patient' – both the noun and the adjective – are derived from the same Latin root, *patiens*, which describes a person who must bear or undergo something (suffering or treatment). From the same Latin stem *pati*, we also get the words 'passion' and 'passive'. In Christian tradition, the 'Passion of Christ' is commonly used to mean Jesus' suffering on the cross; but the root meaning of passion is not strictly about suffering. Rather, it means passively undergoing something imposed by external circumstances or people. Exploring these roots, W. H. Vanstone describes a patient as 'one who is done to, is treated … aware of the dependence of his own destiny upon what is decided and done by others'.[9] He paints a vivid picture of the dependence of a patient: 'He is lifted by the crew of an ambulance, transported to hospital, examined by doctors, monitored by machines, eased by injections, sustained by intravenous drip, reassured by nurses, visited by friends.'[10]

Vanstone himself was thrown into the role of patient in his mid 50s, when he suffered a heart attack. Four years later, his best-selling work of popular theology was published, *The Stature of Waiting*. Perhaps something of his own experience of being a patient had led him to reflect on the nature of passivity, dependence and patience, and to argue, as we shall see, for the dignity of waiting.

We don't like to wait. As the former hospice chaplain Bob Whorton writes, 'Waiting seems to be a defeat for my ego.'[11] Our world values speed, efficiency, achievement and control. When my wife's cousin suffered a stroke, we raced across town to pay him a visit. We found him lying alone in a room with the curtains closed. He was unable to sit up. His speech was slurred. I pulled up a chair. We had little to say. We sat together in silence, while my mind scanned the remaining tasks of the day and reordered them to make the doing of them more efficient. I felt uncomfortable, not only because of the awkwardness between us, but also because I was all too aware that at any time I could be consigned to this world of shaded windows and endless waiting.

Once again, we are dealing with loss and the inevitability of grieving the life we knew and the autonomy we enjoyed. Whether there is any potential in this place of waiting and dependence remains to be seen.

Dying

One further loss of independence – the ultimate one – is encountered in the process of dying. Long before a person is actively dying, they may have received a diagnosis of an incurable illness. They find themselves on a journey they did not ask to undertake. As the journey progresses, autonomy may give way to increasing dependence.

In my work, I support people with incurable or 'terminal' illnesses. While this news can feel devastating for some, it can also feel somewhat unreal and theoretical for as long as a person believes that they might live with the condition indefinitely. An incurable illness might still be treatable. Life has a terminus for all of us; but we habitually take refuge in the comfort of an indefinite horizon and the feeling that we still have options. The hospice patient sitting opposite me might have been labelled 'terminal', but who's to say I will live longer than they?

Yet for people with an incurable illness, there is often a day when their world changes; a new scan reveals that their disease has progressed and they have been told, more or less explicitly, they have not got long. On the calendar of their lives, death has been pencilled in. At this point, our work often changes: our conversation becomes more intimate. I don't subscribe to the 'blank screen' approach of classical psychotherapy; but even so, something may fall away between us. We become conscious that somewhere, out of earshot, a clock is ticking. Whether or not their journey will require complex palliative care, they are now dependent on the unfolding of a process over which they have little control.

This loss of autonomy may be accompanied by acute feelings, including physical pain, fear, loneliness, sadness, anger, helplessness, uncertainty and dread. However, for some, it is the loss of control that is hardest to bear. After Canada decriminalized assisted dying in 2016, one study found that the main reason people requested medical assistance to end their lives was *loss of autonomy*; not, as we might have supposed, the wish to avoid pain or other symptoms, which few respondents mentioned.[12] It is further evidence that we don't fear death so much as we fear dependence.

Progressive disability, ageing, illness and dying are forms of loss that leave us dependent and with limited control. The life we knew shrinks; processes and people take over. Perhaps we have lived our lives like a seasoned mariner, sailing single-handedly around the globe, needing no one, with our hands firmly at the helm. The forfeiture of autonomy and independence from these inevitable forms of loss can feel devastating. As well as coping with the adjustment to a restricted lifestyle, we may need to grieve a whole range of activities that are no longer open to us. I have often come across people who have been active outdoors, climbing mountains or playing sports, whose illness now prevents them from doing these things. There is much to grieve and, sometimes, precious little time in which to do it. When I was a health-care chaplain, I was once called to support a family at the hospital bedside of a man whose cancer had been discovered late. He had died after a short illness. His sister shook her head in disbelief as she said, 'Eight weeks ago, he completed a marathon.'

In the face of such circumstances, what is there but loss? Can there be anything transformative in the loss of independence and autonomy that can strike at any time of life, and that becomes increasingly inevitable through the life course? The grief that accompanies progressive disability, ageing, illness and dying cries out to be acknowledged; the road ahead seems pocked with pain. Can there be spiritual transformation amid the grief of dependence?

Dependence and spiritual transformation

Reframing dependence

One of the most astonishing accounts of a life from the perspective of a disabled person is Jean-Dominique Bauby's best-selling *The Diving Bell and the Butterfly*. Bauby was 43 years old, and at the height of his career as Editor-in-Chief of the French magazine *Elle*, when he suffered a massive stroke. He was left with locked-in syndrome: neither able to move nor communicate with the outside world, except by moving one eyelid. With this one eyelid, he was able to tell his story. I bought his book years ago but left it unread. His predicament seemed too awful to contemplate; it conjured up my worst nightmare.

Despite his situation, Bauby remained himself: shrewd, self-aware, wry and curious. His body still felt pain, even though he was pinned down by it, as if wearing a heavy diving suit. His mind, however, floated free. 'My mind takes flight like a butterfly,' he wrote. 'There is so much to do. You can wander off in space or in time, set out for Tierra del Fuego or for King Midas' court.'[13]

Elsewhere, he described himself being buoyed up by 'small slices of life, these small gusts of happiness', such as came from the letters of friends: 'roses picked at dusk, the laziness of a rainy Sunday'.[14] He revelled in an outing by the seaside that allowed him to smell the aroma of grilled steak. At other times, the grief was raw. Playing the game hangman with his ten-year-old son, he reported: 'Grief surges over me ... I, his father, have lost the simple right to ruffle his bristly hair, clasp his downy neck, hug his small, lithe, warm body tight against me.'

There was no way of sanitizing his experience: 'My condition is monstrous, iniquitous, revolting, horrible.'[15] Yet, despite all, he testified to emotional and spiritual survival in the most extreme circumstances. It was an extraordinary gift.

Bauby's story rubs our noses in the worst-case scenario, in turns terrifying and astonishing, tossing us the beautiful slivers of life that remain to him. For me, his account functions as a kind of imaginative backstop. What is the worst that dependence can throw at us? It allows us to imagine an unimaginable life. While we would not wish it on anyone, we know it can be lived. After reading Bauby's account, the fear of progressive physical limitations diminishes; the wonder at life's sheer gift expands.

A different way of reframing dependence is to recognize its intrinsic value. As we saw earlier, Vanstone's experience of dependence led him to write about the 'stature of waiting'. Pointing to a world that valorizes enterprise, productivity and initiative, he argues for the dignity of receiving, perceiving and waiting. He, too, uses the image of the butterfly. As if anticipating Bauby, he imagines 'a man of great achievement lying, at the end of his life, blind, immobile, and almost totally helpless upon his bed'. He argues that beauty appears in the world when a butterfly's wing is 'seen', and its beauty actualized in a human mind. 'So when a man receives and recognizes the beauty of a butterfly's wing he is no less enriching the totality of the world than when, by art and skill, he creates … a thing of equal beauty.'[16]

For Vanstone, the dignity of dependence is rooted in the example of Jesus, who allowed himself to become a passive victim, subject to the murderous authorities of his day. From this, he argues that God, in Jesus, 'hands himself over' to the world. Therefore, human beings, made in the image of God, must see their dignity 'not only in being a point of activity in the world but also in being a point of receptivity'. The image of God in humanity means that he 'must not see it as degrading that he should wait upon the world, be helped, be provided for, be dependent; for as such he is, by God's gift, what God Himself makes Himself to be'.[17] In short, receiving is no less God-like than achieving.

From the waiting God, it is a short step to the disabled God. Nancy Eiesland described her longing for a divine intervention that would speak to her, a disabled person. 'But my epiphany bore little resemblance to the God I was expecting or the God of my dreams,' she wrote. Instead, 'I saw God in a sip-puff wheelchair, that is, the chair used mostly by quadriplegics enabling them to maneuver by blowing and sucking on a strawlike device.'[18] This image of God reframed her disability. She came to see that religious institutions had often contributed to her invisibility and marginalization by their theology. For Eiesland, the disabled God is revealed in the resurrection of Jesus, whose visible and invisible wounds are there for the disciples to witness. Jesus must have hobbled from the tomb. If Jesus' resurrected body gives us a glimpse or foretaste of the new humanity he promised after death, then it is clear that this humanity incorporates physical disability. This insight places disabled people at the heart of human community and challenges others to learn from their humanity. It is a liberatory insight that invites each of us to come to the disabled God, *just as I am*.

Falling upward

We have seen how the losses we experience because of progressive disability may be reframed. But how might the grief we feel at ageing bring with it greater connection, insight or growth?

St Paul, writing to the church in Corinth in the first century, observes a see-saw action in the human life course: 'Even though our outer nature is wasting away, our inner nature is being renewed day by day' (2 Cor. 4.16). Physical decline, as we accumulate the years, may be mirrored by spiritual renewal. Although Paul was directly addressing a Christian congregation, he is touching on a universal truth: as we grow older, we both lose and gain. In the midst of grieving for our diminishing faculties, health, independence and opportunities, there may be a widening horizon of our inner worlds.

This see-saw action was described by Carl Jung in terms of the 'two halves of life'. He likened the human life course to the trajectory of the sun across the sky. Childhood and youth occupy the morning, midday represents a tipping point, with the 'afternoon of life' and old age to follow. For Jung, the most significant stages are the middle two: youth, from puberty to about age 40, and the 'afternoon of life' that immediately follows.

In the first half of life, he suggests, we spend our energy '[striking] our roots in the world':[19] pursuing money, success, career, reputation, family and status. In the second half of life, we face the challenge of making meaning from these endeavours. The transition between these two halves of life can be stormy. In popular consciousness, it is the period of the 'midlife crisis', where we sense our options contracting and begin to develop a new relationship to death. Metaphorically, we are 'over the hill'. What we could once happily ignore is now laid out in full view: the road that runs down to the sea.

Jung wrote that for men around the age of 40, 'Statistics show a rise in the frequency of mental depressions.'[20] The task of the second half of life, if we are to avoid becoming 'niggards, pedants, applauders of the past or else eternal adolescents', is 'the illumination of the self', Jung suggests. 'We cannot live the afternoon of life according to the programme of life's morning; for what was great in the morning will be little at evening, and what in the morning was true will at evening have become a lie.'[21]

The second half of life is an invitation to relinquish the ego-building projects that served us well in the first half of life, when our aim was to establish an independent self in the world. 'The first task', writes Richard Rohr, 'is to build a strong "container" or identity; the second is to find the contents that the container was meant to hold.'[22] He describes this movement into the second half of life as 'falling upward', an evocative paradox that hints at the possibility that ageing holds both grief and promise.

Jung argues that human beings would not live into their 70s or 80s if their advanced years were not significant for the species. The afternoon of life, therefore, 'cannot be merely a pitiful appendage to life's morning'.[23] Even as we grieve the passing of our youthful bodies, easy health and the illusion of limitless possibilities, there are dormant seeds stirring in the human soul. The transformation is not automatic; but the invitation is there. It is an invitation to reconsider our values, embracing what may seem strange and contradictory – what Jung terms the 'dualistic state' – rather than a rigid and fearful clinging to the past. It is an invitation to take up our seats as elders among our people, shifting our focus from competition and attainment to nurturing others in our community. It is an invitation to look squarely at death and, in realizing our finitude, to rediscover the preciousness of life. It is an invitation to attend to our crumbling body – 'brother ass' as St Francis affectionately called it – and become more aware of our embodied nature, and more grounded in the world.

Many writers have captured something of the paradox of 'falling upward'. Erikson describes the final stage of his 'eight ages of man' as 'ego-integrity', characterized by seeing the world as meaningful, and having some 'spiritual sense'.[24] James Fowler applied the insights of Erikson, among others, to construct his 'stages of faith'. The last of these he describes as 'universalizing faith', reminiscent of Jung's 'dualistic state'. People whose faith reaches this stage have gone beyond being concerned with the protection of their own traditions. They possess 'a radical commitment to justice and love and of selfless passion for a transformed world'.[25] Aldous Huxley offers a slightly different vision of universalizing faith, which places contemplation before action as the ultimate goal of human life. He explores the 'Perennial Philosophy': the skein of shared insights that runs through many religious and philosophical traditions. He concludes, 'In all the historic formulations of the Perennial Philosophy it is axiomatic that the end of human life is contemplation, or the direct and intuitive awareness of God.'[26] Falling upward, in these terms, involves allowing our attention to turn to contemplation of the transcendent and what the mystics have described as the inner gaze of love.

Whether or not we find such richness of meaning and spiritual connection in our later years, at the very least our ageing souls may gain perspective. Joe Moran writes, 'Here is one compensation of getting older: it turns us into comedians by default ... The middle-aged are converts to life's essential absurdity.'[27] The recognition of the absurdity of our first-half-of-life preoccupations can be an important step in letting go of ego-projects and learning to embrace the gifts and griefs of ageing.

In ageing, then, we encounter dependence. It may be that we become physically dependent on others for our basic needs. But even if we live independently to the very end of our lives, we remain subject to the inexorable changes that take place in the human psyche over the life course. We didn't ask to be on this train; we didn't choose the stations or the final destination. As we accumulate the years, the train passes over the hill and thunders into the afternoon of life, the rails now visible as a silver thread vanishing to the setting sun. Our finitude is laid bare before us. In this new vista, there is loss and promise, grief and grace, and the invitation to inward renewal.

Confinement and creativity

We have seen how disability and ageing can leave us dependent and grieving the life we once knew; and that, while the losses are real, they are not the whole story. What, then, of the two other forms of dependence we have been considering in this chapter: illness and dying? Is there anything in the confinement these impose on us that can issue an invitation to greater connection, insight or growth?

Once again, it is important not to romanticize the experience of serious or terminal illness. People who are suffering do not need the added burden of living up to some heroic ideal or searching for silver linings. If we are to find anything transformative in this kind of grief, it will probably surprise us, coming upon us as an unexpected gift.

For some, illness takes them into a liminal space where they experience an inner realignment. Donald Eadie was forced into three long periods of convalescence following spinal operations to tackle a degenerative disc disease. This meant taking early retirement and being confronted with losing not only his health but also his identity and role. Reflecting on this period, he observed:

> I am learning that sometimes within our loss and grieving, disappointments and rage, fears and tears there is a loosening, a cracking open and fresh flowing of life, a freedom permitting a deeper yet hidden realignment, and a joyful inner homecoming. These experiences are essentially intermingling, not to be held as separate.[28]

During one period in hospital, he began to reflect on 'those territories of human experience that frighten us – the dark, negative and destructive'. It was a puzzle to him why, for some, something deep within us permits these 'to be not only recognised and owned but somehow mysteriously transformed'. Again, he stresses the 'both/and' nature of this experience: 'The reality may not be removed; however, it becomes the context for deepening and growing.'[29]

For others, the confinement of illness seems to nurture creative potential. The Orkney poet George Mackay Brown contracted tuberculosis as a teenager. In his twentieth year, he spent six months in hospital, 'in the little sanatorium, set high on a brae above Kirkwall'. Remarkably, he wrote:

> In some ways I was actually grateful for the tubercle. It saved me from the world of 'getting and spending' that I had dreaded so much ... I even exulted that I had been branded with the same illness as Keats, Stevenson, Emily Brontë, Francis Thompson, D. H. Lawrence.[30]

In the decade that followed, his poetic gift was nurtured in the spacious mornings he spent in bed.

> My mother would bring me breakfast upstairs on a tray – tea and toast and an egg: a ritual that I'm sure caused many a

one to say, 'That lazy brute! All he does is drink and sleep half the day ... As for me, I was writing my small poems, and reading books.'[31]

Of course, there is no guarantee that the confinement of illness will bear fruit. We may be simply too ill to benefit. Further, as Allan Kellehear has said of suffering, 'at its existential root it is about grief and loss'.[32] Its grief must be borne and worked through like any other. Yet, in the midst of grief, the relief from daily responsibilities and from the grinding round of 'getting and spending' can turn up an unexpected gift. It is perhaps the same thing we go looking for when we go on retreat or pilgrimage: the new hope or perspective that emerges when we voluntarily down tools and pay attention to our inner lives.

The art of dying

Perhaps the ultimate confinement is experienced by those who are at the end of life. People approaching this stage tell me how difficult it is to be feeling increasingly ill or in pain knowing that, this time, they are not going to get better. We are fortunate in the UK that we have advanced forms of palliative medicine available to help keep patients as comfortable as possible in their final days. But the question of *how* we should die remains awkward. Is the process of dying something we should try to get through as swiftly and painlessly as possible or are there gifts to be discovered, even as the hourglass spills its final grains? Confronted with the loss of everything and everyone we know, can it make any sense to speak of spirituality, namely the possibility of connection, insight and even growth?

Kellehear finds some evidence that the process of dying may, surprisingly, offer just this: 'Existing studies of the human dying experience suggest that the road to death tends to erode habit, pretense, preconception and even fear in one's usual character to reveal deeper and novel experiences in personal direction, positive purpose, and social intimacy.'[33]

Irvin Yalom, who worked with cancer patients at the end of life, 'found that many of them, rather than succumb to numbing despair, were positively and dramatically transformed'.[34] He saw their deeper communication, stronger appreciation of life, and their reordering of priorities by 'trivializing life's trivia'.

In the summer of 2023, Simon Boas discovered he had cancer. He was in his mid 40s. In September of that year, he wrote an article for the *Jersey Evening Post*, where he set out some ways in which cancer had clarified his thoughts: 'Important things: love; kindness; meaning. Not important: money; status; validation.'[35] In the final few months of his life, he gathered his experience into a book, *A Beginner's Guide to Dying*. For Boas, the biggest help to him in reflecting on death has been the ability – that he believes most of us have – to sort out what is important in life and what is not. 'Death is a wonderful putter-of-things-into-perspective.'[36] One of the transforming values he discovered in his dying months was – paradoxically – gratitude. He had learnt to compare himself with others, not 'upwards' but 'downwards'. Comparing his 46 years of life to the lives of most people throughout history, he felt he had won the lottery. Complaining that he was dying, he suggested, was 'as churlish as complaining I've had to share a £92 million lottery prize with another winning ticket'.[37]

These observations from a sociologist, psychiatrist and cancer patient suggest the possibility of the late flowering of the human soul, even as the winter of death approaches. The fruits of spirituality seem abundant: greater connection with loved ones, renewed insight into what truly matters, and personal growth, even at the end. I have come across many stories at the end of life: of estranged partners reunited; cruel mothers becoming warm and attentive; and siblings seeing one another in a new way. For others, the fruit has been the simple acceptance of death, the ability to relinquish projects and plans, and even the grace to say goodbye to loved ones. As the former hospice chaplain Bob Whorton observes, 'There are often rich blessings on this part of the journey as well as intense emotional pain.'[38]

Perhaps this late flowering should not surprise us: for centuries, in western Europe, death was seen as an opportunity for spiritual growth. It was interpreted within the framework of the *ars moriendi*, the medieval 'art of dying', a tradition that held out the possibility of a 'good death'. In the wake of the Black Death in fourteenth-century Europe, woodcuts were manufactured that depicted demons on one side of the bed of the dying person, and angels and saints on the other. Death was a tug of war for the soul of the dying.

These medieval images are strong stuff: but, at root, the *ars moriendi* underlines that the dying have choices about how to frame their dying. The dying may need skilled people who can help them reflect on the kinds of questions that dying brings to the fore. Carlo Leget has reinterpreted the *ars moriendi* for the context of contemporary spiritual care at the end of life. He suggests a number of questions dying people may confront, such as 'Who am I and what do I really want? How do I cope with suffering? How do I say goodbye? How do I look back on my life? What can I hope for?'[39] These are universal questions (and not ones only asked by people from particular faith communities) that point to the kind of spiritual concerns that deserve attention at the end of life.

Progressive disability, illness, ageing and dying are universal forms of loss that may leave us experiencing significant grief. Common to them all is the decline of autonomy and independence. Typically, we take these for granted till we find them being taken away. These losses are woven into the human story; and, at first sight, they paint a bleak picture of what lies ahead for most of our race. Yet, as we have seen, the very fact that such losses are universal – part of the fabric of human existence – raises the question of whether there might be more to later life than unrelenting woe. In the midst of our grief for our diminishing lives, there may come an invitation to spiritual transformation: the experience of renewed connection, insight and personal growth.

Notes

1 M. McCartney, 2014, *Living with Dying*, London: Pinter & Martin, p. 198.
2 C. Watson, 2019, *The Language of Kindness: A nurse's story*, London: Vintage, p. 279.
3 Atul Gawande, 2015, *Being Mortal: Illness, medicine, and what matters in the end*, London: Wellcome Collection, p. 55.
4 S. Roos, 2017, *Chronic Sorrow*, London: Routledge.
5 C. Fenner, 2020, 'Just as I Am, without One Plea', Hymnology Archive (revised 26 Feb. 2024), at https://www.hymnologyarchive.com/just-as-i-am, accessed 14.04.2025.
6 Quoted in S. Davey, 2004, 'Just As I Am ...': The life of Charlotte Elliott, at https://www.christianstudylibrary.org/article/just-i-am-%E2%80%A6-life-charlotte-elliott, accessed 23.07.2025.
7 Stewart Henderson, a poet, song lyricist and broadcaster, collaborated with singer-songwriter Yvonne Lyon on the lyrics of this song. I am grateful to them for permission to quote the title here.
8 M. de Montaigne, 1877, 'That to Study Philosophy is to Learn to Die', trans. C. Cotton, in W. Carew Hazlitt, ed., *Essays of Michel de Montaigne*, London: Reeves and Turner, at https://www.gutenberg.org/ebooks/3600, accessed 14.04.2025.
9 W. H. Vanstone, 1982, *The Stature of Waiting*, London: Darton, Longman and Todd, p. 35.
10 Vanstone, *Stature of Waiting*, p. 34.
11 B. Whorton, 2015, *Voices from the Hospice*, London: SCM Press, p. 86.
12 M. Li, S. Watt, M. Escaf, M. Gardam, A. Heesters, G. O'Leary and G. Rodin, 'Medical Assistance in Dying: Implementing a hospital-based program in Canada', *New England Journal of Medicine*, 376/21 (2017), pp. 2082–8, at https://www.nejm.org/doi/10.1056/NEJmms1700606, accessed 14.04.2025.
13 J.-D. Bauby, 1998, *The Diving Bell and the Butterfly*, trans. J. Leggatt, London: Fourth Estate, p. 13.
14 Bauby, *Diving Bell*, p. 91.
15 Bauby, *Diving Bell*, p. 79.
16 Vanstone, *Stature of Waiting*, pp. 112–13.
17 Vanstone, *Stature of Waiting*, p. 112.
18 N. L. Eiesland, 1994, *The Disabled God: Toward a liberatory theology of disability*, Nashville, TN: Abingdon Press, p. 89.
19 C. G. Jung, 1975, *Structure and Dynamics of the Psyche: The collected works of C. G. Jung*, vol. 8, trans. R. F. C. Hull, Princeton: Princeton University Press, p. 509, at https://jungiancenter.org/wp-con

tent/uploads/2023/09/vol-8-the-structure-and-dynamics-of-the-psyche.pdf, accessed 14.04.2025.

20 Jung, *Structure and Dynamics*, p. 511.

21 Jung, *Structure and Dynamics*, p. 517.

22 R. Rohr, 2011, *Falling Upward: A spirituality for the two halves of life*, San Francisco, CA: Jossey-Bass, p. xiii.

23 Jung, *Structure and Dynamics*, p. 517.

24 E. H. Erikson, 1965, *Childhood and Society*, 2nd ed., Harmondsworth: Penguin, p. 260.

25 J. W. Fowler, 1981, *Stages of Faith: The psychology of human development and the quest for meaning*, New York, NY: Harper & Row, pp. 200–1.

26 A. Huxley, 1946, *The Perennial Philosophy*, London: Chatto & Windus, p. 337.

27 J. Moran, 2021, *If You Should Fail: Why success eludes us and why it doesn't matter*, London: Penguin, p. 142.

28 D. Eadie, 2019, *Into the Foothills of Transformation*, Glasgow: Wild Goose Publications, p. 11.

29 Eadie, *Foothills of Transformation*, p. 20.

30 G. M. Brown, 1997, *For the Islands I Sing*, London: John Murray, p. 58.

31 Brown, *For the Islands*, p. 73.

32 A. Kellehear, 2014, *The Inner Life of the Dying Person*, New York, NY: Columbia University Press, p. 17.

33 Kellehear, *Inner Life*, p. 13.

34 I. D. Yalom, 2008, *Staring at the Sun: Being at peace with your own mortality*, London: Piatkus, p. 34.

35 Boas, S. (2024), *A Beginner's Guide to Dying*, London: Swift Press, p. 13.

36 Boas, *Beginner's Guide*, p. 33.

37 Boas, *Beginner's Guide*, p. 50.

38 Whorton, *Voices from the Hospice*, p. 16.

39 C. Leget, 2017, *Art of Living, Art of Dying*, London: Jessica Kingsley Publisher.

4

Parting

> Love is proved in the letting go.
> (C. Day-Lewis, 'Walking Away')¹

It is one of my earliest memories. I was perhaps two years old. The doorbell rang at home, and my mother welcomed in a strange woman. My pram was standing in the hallway, a boxy chariot as tall as I was, with a fold-down canopy of navy blue fabric, and four huge wheels, with solid rubber tyres. The spokes were still shiny; you could see your face in the tiny wheel caps. The adults chatted. Then, without warning, the stranger took hold of the handle and began to wheel it out, through the front door. Instantly, I realized: I was losing my pram.

I remember clinging to it with all my strength, screaming at my mother not to let it go. She prised me away and held me aside until the woman had left. I stood, tearful and enraged, unable to calm down, shouting at my mother that I wanted it back – my pram. Perhaps it represented safety and the privilege of being wheeled around. Perhaps it signified my mother and her warm, nurturing cocoon. Now I was in the brave new world of toddlerdom, a life of bruises and tantrums, and being left on my own to play. Although I can't have been using it for months, I knew there was no going back.

Letting go

Life is a series of partings. When our first child was born, my wife commented, 'It's letting go from now on.' It was a profound comment and little did I realize its enormity. Partings can be agony; and the serial partings of family life bring joy and sorrow in abundance. It may be that deep-breath moment when our children are dropped at nursery for the first time, when we hope not to convey our anxiety to them. Or it may be their last day, when we sense a chapter closing.

I remember going to pick up our youngest daughter from her nursery on her final day. Parents watched the end-of-year sing-along and then bumped elbows in the cloakroom, trying to make sure that nothing was left behind. I sat on a low bench, with my daughter on my knee, chatting away, as I pulled on her blue canvas shoes that had the cherry motif and silver buckle. I knew I was doing this for the last time. Soon she would be at 'big school', with different shoes, and a relationship with me that would be ever so slightly different. I sat with tears wetting my cheeks. I made no attempt to hide them; in any case, I was not alone in my grief.

I suspect many parents will recognize these feelings, which are repeated over and over in the ordinary course of family life, and in the biography of a growing family. Perhaps they reach their zenith when a child leaves home, when we may feel as if a light has gone out. I have a focal memory of waving goodbye to my son as he stood in the doorway of the train that would take him 400 miles away, to London and to university for the first time. Fixing his smile, he waved back and turned to go. My wife and I walked back down the platform, picking our way past iron pillars that loomed in our blurry vision.

For years I had anticipated this moment. I had stuck a copy of C. Day-Lewis's poem 'Walking Away' on the wall beside my desk at home. My hunch was that I would need it. In the poem, Day-Lewis describes the experience of watching his son walking away at the end of his first football match, at the start of a new school year.

> It is eighteen years ago, almost to the day –
> A sunny day with leaves just turning,
> The touch-lines new-ruled – since I watched you play

PARTING

> Your first game of football, then, like a satellite
> Wrenched from its orbit, go drifting away
>
> Behind a scatter of boys. I can see
> You walking away from me towards the school
> With the pathos of a half-fledged thing set free
> Into a wilderness, the gait of one
> Who finds no path where the path should be.
>
> That hesitant figure, eddying away
> Like a winged seed loosened from its parent stem,
> Has something I never quite grasp to convey
> About nature's give-and-take – the small, the scorching
> Ordeals which fire one's irresolute clay.

In the final stanza, Day-Lewis reflects on the meaning of this 'ordeal':

> I have had worse partings, but none that so
> Gnaws at my mind still. Perhaps it is roughly
> Saying what God alone could perfectly show –
> How selfhood begins with a walking away,
> And love is proved in the letting go.[2]

There are two truths here that tug at each other. One is that parting hurts. The unspoken experience for Day-Lewis on the touchline is that the 'hesitant figure, eddying away / Like a winged seed loosened from its parent stem', seems to have briefly forgotten his watching father. He does not return to the touchline to say goodbye; nor does he look for a word of approval or guidance. The seed has flown; and the watching father is left to wonder if he has given him enough to navigate the world on his own.

The second truth is that this is a necessary loss. It is only in such experiences that selfhood can be freed to fly. The grieving father is confronted by love's hard edges. Love is 'proved' in the letting go – a deliberate double meaning which suggests that love is both demonstrated and tested in this act of generous freeing.

Parting is a painful but necessary loss that is a universal human experience. Judith Viorst describes the 'necessary losses' that accompany us from cradle to grave.[3] While these partings invoke pain, it is often more painful for the one letting go than for the one being let go. Children leaving home for a new job or a college education may feel anxious; but they also may feel euphoric as they step out into new experiences and relationships, making the transition towards mature selfhood and an independent identity. By contrast, the parents who wave them off may step back inside to face an empty house, the drudgery of everyday life, and each other.

The 'empty nest' is, of course, only one kind of parting; but its grief seems to be significantly under-reported. Perhaps this is true of necessary losses in general. We don't expect much sympathy for partings that are nearly universal, and that seem necessary milestones in the course of life. Yet transitions, such as the first day of school or the 'empty nest', can feel like a death and provoke strong grief feelings.

As Day-Lewis's poem suggests, the worse alternative to letting go is *not* letting go. In Susan Cain's *Bittersweet*, she chronicles a painful chapter in her own life when she left her mother and went off to college. As the youngest child, she had experienced an Edenic existence, with her omnipotent mother attending to her every need. As a teenager, this attention became suffocating: her mother insisted she follow an 'ironclad code', involving rules about religion, boys and friendships. When Cain inevitably broke the rules, her mother's reaction was volatile: 'Waves of anger, floods of tears; days, then weeks, of stony silence.' Then, eventually, since they could not bear to be separated, they made up. 'We would hug, shed a few tears; I would lower myself gratefully into her warm bath of love and comfort.'[4]

As this cycle repeated, Cain began to long for the day when she could escape to college. Eventually, she found herself at Princeton; free at last, except for the dorm telephone that enabled her mother to make frequent checks on her. Cain worked out her independence by keeping diaries, in which she recorded her own transgressions in detail and her mother's increasingly intrusive attempts to maintain control. She chronicled her love–hate feelings towards her mother and her dawning grief at the realization that the warm, nurturing mother of her pre-school days no longer existed and, perhaps, had never existed.

The diaries piled up; the first year ended. Her parents came to help her pack up her things and bring them home. She would follow a few days later. As they were leaving, she had a sudden impulse to offload the pile of diaries onto her mother, for her to take home 'for safekeeping'. In that moment, she believed her mother, once again, to be the warm, nurturing mother of her infancy: someone who would not stoop to read the private diaries of another. Later, she came to see this as a murderous act: her unconscious freeing her by putting this relationship to death. When she returned home a few days later, her mother appeared in a doorway with the diaries, miming a guillotine blade across her neck. It was over. In the years that followed, their relationship remained civil; but the former connection had gone.

Although this parting involved a sudden and dramatic act, with far-reaching consequences, it is a familiar enough transition: young adults separating from their family of origin to develop an independent identity. There are clearly choices to be made, both for leavers and for those who let them go. In these losses lie the potential for spiritual transformation: new connections, insight and growth. Cain's experience illustrates, in an extreme way, what can happen when the fear of losing someone drowns out grief's quiet invitation to spiritual transformation. It reveals the shadow side: an unspiritual catalogue of compulsion, fear, control and blindness to the needs of the other.

Not every parting is as lop-sided as the parent–child relationship. We frequently experience the parting of peers, as when a group comes to an end, a relationship breaks up, couples separate or a holiday is over. These endings can be like little deaths;

and, like death, we often cope by trying to deny them. At the end of a school career, tearful teenagers sign each other's shirts in permanent ink, swap social-media handles and swear to keep in touch. Group members compile contact lists or assure one another that their paths are bound to cross. Others slink away into the shadows, feeling they never belonged in the first place. We cope with partings as best we can.

It is rare that we part cleanly. Partings may bring up for us deep existential anxieties: the fear of abandonment, the passing of time, the transitory nature of all experience or the inevitability of death. It takes some courage to look another person in the eye, to invite a handshake or a hug, and to say, with some firmness, goodbye – as my first therapist did to me after our final session, at the end of nearly three years of work together. *Goodbye.* This felt like a clean, honest, adult ending that was, as we say in the business, part of the work. That did not prevent me from experiencing the parting as a loss. Fifteen years later, I still feel the pull to go back to him.

The spirituality of parting

So far, I have suggested a working definition of spirituality as 'that which fosters *connection, insight and growth*'. In what ways, then, might the grief of parting help to nurture these qualities in us? If there is such a thing as a spirituality of loss, what might it look like in the context of painful parting?

Leaving

Where parting is a 'necessary loss', such as with the example of the 'empty nest', the invitation of grief to spiritual transformation is perhaps clearest. Children leaving home, saying goodbye to 'good-enough parents', have a life to lead on their own terms. This can be a daunting and exciting time. Leaving the comfort and familiarity of home for strange surroundings, diverse people, and the challenge of a university course or a new job, can leave young people feeling ambivalent: torn between the desire to stay and to go. The grief of leaving can be palpable, as young people come to terms with the fact that the door of childhood is closing behind them. Of course, some will be relieved to get away from home and, increasingly, many will return after tertiary education or never move out in the first place. The 2021 census in England and Wales revealed that the median age for adult children living with their parents is 24 years old; in London it is 25.[5] Leaving home is increasingly a stage of life, rather than an event.

The grief of parting holds out an invitation that can be thought of as a series of tasks. Young people leaving home have the task of loosening the bonds with their family of origin and making new connections with strangers. They have the task of negotiating a new identity, deciding what they will cherish of the past and what they will leave behind. Bound up with this is the task of forging their own values and setting their moral compass in the direction of the mature self they would like to become. These are just some of the ways in which the necessary loss of growing up and leaving home issues an invitation to new connection, insight and growth.

Being alone

One important aspect of forging connections is the new relationship each of us must make with our own selves. Parting leaves us each alone with our self, even if only momentarily. It confronts us with profound existential questions: 'Who am I in the absence of others? Will I "hold it together" or will I fall apart? Am I ultimately alone?'

In a paper with the evocative title *The Capacity to Be Alone*, paediatrician Donald Winnicott explored how we typically develop this capacity from early in life, noting that 'the capacity to be alone is ... nearly synonymous with emotional maturity'.[6] This 'sophisticated aloneness' is achieved only by first being alone in the presence of someone for a considerable period of time: a 'good-enough mother', whose care and attention may be internalized and carried within the child as a growing sense of possessing a capable and independent self. The infant who crawls or shuffles into the next room, away from the parent, must momentarily consider whether, out of sight, that parent still exists. A young child typically learns to internalize a sense or image of 'mother' (or whoever is the primary caregiver); it is this *internal* presence of the caregiver that allows the child to stray for a while. As we have seen, in the context of bereavement, this process has central significance for how we cope with our grief and perhaps encounter its transforming potential.

It is when we part from someone significant that our gaze turns inward. 'Can I do this on my own?' we ask ourselves. Another way we might unconsciously frame this question is, 'Have I imbibed enough of this person to carry them within me?' In the absence of our caregivers, parting causes us to look inwards and perhaps draw on the people we have internalized. For years after ending with my first therapist, I discovered I could have ongoing conversations with him in my head, which felt nearly as fruitful as the therapy sessions themselves. Odd metaphors he had suggested, which had made no sense at the time, came back to me full of meaning. I had developed an internal image of him – an 'inner therapist' – with whom a dialogue could continue.

Learning to cope with being alone is not only an emotional task but also an existential one. Irvin Yalom has written widely on the existential dimension in psychotherapy. He observes different types of isolation in human experience. These include social, or 'interpersonal', isolation and the '*intra*personal' isolation we experience when we become cut off from parts of our self, such as being unable to access our feelings or own our desires. He also identifies a third type – existential isolation – that he defines as 'an unbridgeable gulf between oneself and any other being'.[7] This gulf exists whether we part from others or not. It is the isolation of being the only person who can wholly inhabit our body, walk in our shoes, feel our pain and die our death. Parting exposes our predicament. It thrusts us into the spotlight on an empty stage, speaking our soliloquy to the darkness. In this moment, we are confronted with our existential aloneness.

In such austere and terrifying moments, we may feel close to despair. The grief of parting can feel overwhelming. Yet the invitation remains. While sitting in a lonely room in a strange city, we may discover inner strengths of which we were previously unaware. We may find a new circle of people and new values that animate our truest selves. We may discern the budding and flowering of a latent identity that had been waiting for this time to emerge. Away from the boxing effect of friends' and family's versions of us, we can discover a new freedom to be.

Moving on

Leaving is one kind of loss; letting go is another. As we have seen, the moment of a child leaving home can provoke powerful feelings of grief for parents and younger siblings, which may be felt for decades. Families come in all shapes and sizes, of course, and the true picture is complex. But for parents, in particular, the empty nest throws up some profound questions that may, at first, crouch only at the edge of awareness. As the front door closes on two people who may have spent a quarter of a century bringing up children together, the question arises: 'Who are we now?' The task of renegotiating their relationship lies before them. Closing the door also closes a chapter in their lives. A period of potency is over; in Kahlil Gibran's arresting image, the 'living arrows' have flown.[8] The end of childbearing and child-rearing confronts us with our mortality. From an evolutionary perspective, we have become irrelevant. And as the number around the dinner table shrinks to two, or even one, we may be faced with the painful realization that we have few other meaningful relationships in our lives. An acquaintance, whose youngest child was about to leave home, reflected that he had found love easier to come by than friendship. Our children, siblings, parents, partners will love us, all being well. But friends must be made. By the time our children leave home, the cogs of friendship may be rusty; we may find ourselves reaching for skills we haven't used since the playground. The search for friendship raises an unsettling question: not 'Am I loveable?' but 'Am I likeable?'

If the empty nest shines a searchlight onto our relationships with our partners, our mortality and our friendships (or lack of them), it is perhaps unsurprising if we try to cling to our dependants. The loss of parting is magnified by the realization of these ancillary losses. Our love is indeed 'proved' in the letting go; it is tested to its limits as we wave them off, again and again.

As for leavers, grief holds an invitation for those who let go. The psychoanalyst Erik Erikson famously formulated the 'eight ages of man', the various stages of life at which we face the task of integrating our maturing ego with the reality of the social institutions around us. The seventh age, which lies beyond 'young adulthood', he labels 'generativity'; he defines this as 'the concern in guiding and establishing the next generation'.[9] This stage seems to include the raising of children, but it takes us beyond this to an invitation to a more generous way of being in later life. As Richard Rohr describes it, in the age of generativity, 'I am not preoccupied with collecting more goods and services; quite simply, my desire and effort – every day – is to pay back, to give back to the world a bit of what I have received.'[10] In Erikson's formulation, the opposite of generativity is 'stagnation': a regression to a self-centred and child-like state, perhaps accompanied by an acquired physical or psychological vulnerability that 'becomes the vehicle of self-concern'.

The grief of letting go invites us to make choices: between generativity or stagnation; between connection or isolation; between taking the risk of reinvesting in our loves, friendships and the needs of the world around us or shrinking back into our shell. It invites us to reinterpret our identity: 'If I am no longer a carer of dependent children, then who am I? If I leave the familiar scripts of an abusive partner, what story will I write for myself?' It also invites us to reframe our future, especially when we have made our family our vocation. Even those with busy careers might find that they lose interest in their work after a significant parting, whether a separation, say, or the end of family life.

The age of generativity is also a time when our focus may shift from competition to co-operation. We cease to become the sharp-elbowed employees, borrowers or nursery parents seeking to nudge ahead of the competition for jobs, houses and school places. The grief of letting go (children, career hopes, dreams of a home by the sea) invites us to appreciate what we have; perhaps it leads us to wonder how we can live in a way that brings people together, rather than seeing them as competitors to be fought off. It may turn our attention to our environment: not as a resource to be exploited, but as an heirloom to be treasured for generations to come. Letting go invites us to adopt a focus that is less individualistic and more holistic.

For people of faith, there may be an additional dimension to this call. The realization of our ultimate aloneness, or even the simple loneliness of an empty house, may send us in search of an unseen companion. In Jesus' parable of the lost son, a benevolent father hands over an inheritance to his wayward son, who leaves home and spends all he has on wild living. The father in this story is an exemplar of the truth that 'love is proved in the letting go'. He demonstrates how God can both love us deeply and appear almost absent in his 'hands off' stance towards us. It is only when the son runs out of money – his dreams in tatters – that he comes to his senses. He resolves to return to his father and find work as a servant. The father, who has proved his love in letting his son go, now proves it again in welcoming him back. In the words of the parable, 'while he was still far off, his father saw him and was filled with compassion; he ran and put his arms around him and kissed him' (Luke 15.20, NRSV).

Moments of crisis may be moments of invitation, when we sense a call to connect with something, or someone, greater than ourselves. Amid the cacophony of our busy and preoccupied lives, the quiet call to connect with others, or with an Other, may not be discerned. It is in loss and grief that our world may come to a standstill, and the call can at last be heard.

Notes

1 C. Day-Lewis, 1962, 'Walking Away', in *The Gate*, London: Jonathan Cape.
2 C. Day-Lewis, 1962, 'Walking Away', in *The Gate*, Jonathan Cape. Used by permission of Peters Fraser & Dunlop (www.petersfraserdunlop.com) on behalf of the Estate of C. Day-Lewis.
3 J. Viorst, 1986, *Necessary Losses*, New York: Simon & Schuster.
4 S. Cain, 2023, *Bittersweet: How sorrow and longing make us whole*, New York: Penguin Random House, pp. 6, 7.
5 Office for National Statistics, 2023, 'More Adults Living with Their Parents', at https://www.ons.gov.uk/peoplepopulationandcommunity/populationandmigration/populationestimates/articles/moreadultslivingwiththeirparents/2023-05-10, accessed 14.04.2025.
6 D. W. Winnicott, 1990, *The Maturational Processes and the Facilitating Environment*, London: Karnac Books, p. 31.
7 I. D. Yalom, 1980, *Existential Psychotherapy*, Basic Books, p. 355.
8 K. Gibran, 1923, 'On Children', *The Prophet*, New York, NY: Knopf.
9 E. H. Erikson, 1965, *Childhood and Society*, 2nd ed., Harmondsworth: Penguin, p. 258.
10 R. Rohr, 2011, *Falling Upward: A spirituality for the two halves of life*, San Francisco, CA: Jossey-Bass, p. 121.

5

Nostalgia

Beside one loch, a hind's neat skeleton,
Beside another, a boat pulled high and dry:
Two neat geometries drawn in the weather:
Two things already dead and still to die.

I passed them every summer, rod in hand,
Skirting the bright blue or the spitting gray,
And, every summer, saw how the bleached timbers
Gaped wider and the neat ribs fell away.

Time adds one malice to another one –
Now you'd look very close before you knew
If it's the boat that ran, the hind went sailing.
So many summers, and I have lived them too.

(Norman MacCaig, 'So Many Summers')[1]

I read these words at Alasdair's burial, standing by his grave on a perfect September day. He died suddenly, waiting at his cottage gate for an ambulance. He was 62 years old.

Alasdair was my cousin. He was an ebullient, romantic character, who had travelled the world, worked in the film industry, and had taken early retirement to return to the Highland landscape he had known as a child. In his final decade, he had spent time doing what he loved: fishing and shooting in the wilderness of Sutherland. As with many romantics, there was something restless about him, as if he were searching for a point of stillness he could never quite grasp.

In the poem, Norman MacCaig describes a familiar walk to a favourite fishing spot. Each year, he passes the same abandoned fishing boat and the skeleton of a deer. He notices their 'two neat geometries' and the 'neat ribs' of both that, year by year, fall further into decay. As the years pass, the two become increasingly indistinguishable: an index of his own advancing years, but also a monument to 'so many summers' that he himself lived and enjoyed. The poem seemed right for Alasdair.

Alongside a sense of satisfaction, MacCaig's 'many summers' seem replete with loss. They record time's 'malice' in eroding and conflating memory. They hint at a universal experience of longing to return to a golden past – the weather notwithstanding – that is now slipping away. In short, they evoke *nostalgia*, the Greek roots of which imply the painful yearning for home. Although MacCaig's home was in Edinburgh, it seems he lived for the long summer days when he could return to Lochinver in Assynt – the stage for many of his poems – and take up once more with his friends there.

Nostalgia implies loss. Yet it is a curious kind of loss: a sweet sorrow that is painful and precious all at once. We long to return to places and objects we once knew, frozen in time; and, in the longing, we may find pleasure. How much pleasure we can see in the fact that nostalgia has spawned whole industries: the manufacture of 'retro' objects; the return to simpler technology, such as the resurgence of 'brick' phones and vinyl records; and the trend towards vintage and repurposed products. The fact that nostalgia itself has been commodified points to its enduring power.

Nostalgia seems inherently puzzling. How can wallowing in loss feel enjoyable? What is it that has been lost? And what is contained in our deep desire to recover it? Perhaps we can begin to approach these questions by looking at some of the many faces of nostalgia.

Childhood

One common aspect of nostalgia is the memories of childhood. Alistair McIntosh walked the length of Harris and Lewis in the Western Isles, where he grew up, undertaking a 'journey into land and soul'. Curiously, it was another rotting boat that kindled McIntosh's nostalgia. On passing an old, ruined byre (cowshed), he recalled its glory days of 40 years before. Back then, it was roofed with a sleek, upturned fishing boat. Peering into the ruin, he saw something piled to one side: 'A twisted length of planks, criss-crossed with in-stepped ribs ... lying rotting on the ground. She's slowly growing back into the grass.' He began to wonder about the people who built her, splashing hot tar along her length, filling the spring air with a thick aroma that drifted along the shoreline. 'Oh yes, it's "just" nostalgia,' he commented, 'but curiously I'm also feeling happy that it's come upon me. It opens up a deeper way of seeing.'[2]

Rural nostalgia

For others the sepia tint of nostalgia has a darker edge. James Rebanks, in his chronicle of changing farming practices in Cumbria over three generations, notices another face of nostalgia, in relation to rural life: 'We act as if we popped into town to earn a living a generation or two ago, but will be going home soon to a place in the country.'[3] Here, 'nostalgia' is closer in meaning to its etymology (*nostos* + *algos*): the anguished yearning for home. It is as if we (urban dwellers) feel a profound sense of dislocation, living in a built environment. I wonder if the popularity of SUVs, also known as 'Chelsea tractors', in crowded urban streets embodies this feeling: unconsciously we identify with cars made to look like they belong in a field, complete with four-wheel-drive and scuff-plates at the rear. Many of us seem homesick for the countryside; estate agents tell us that even 'townies' are willing to pay a hefty premium for a sea view. Perhaps we should not be surprised: on an evolutionary timescale, urban living is still a novel experiment, as I will explore in the final chapter. We are, after all, a species that has developed and adapted ourselves over thousands of generations of rural living; our excursion to the city is only recent. The UN estimates that only since 2007 has more than half of the world's population lived in urban settings.[4]

Lost ways of life

Another face of nostalgia is the pathos of a lost way of life. McIntosh reflects on the Clearances that took place in the nineteenth century, when Highland lairds brutally evicted their tenants to make way for more profitable sheep. 'There are no longer any villages between Hushnish and Kinlochresort,' he observes, noting that 'pretty much this whole western coastline of North Harris and South Lewis cries out, laconic in its emptiness.'[5]

The pathos of a clearance village can feel overwhelming, as I discovered recently when I took a side road in Morvern on a whim and found myself parked near the lost township of Inniemore. I wandered among the blackhouse ruins, picturing old women spinning at their doorways, children splashing in the stream, men cutting peat, and women singing together as they washed clothes in rhythmic unison. The name Inniemore[6] resonated with a dim memory, until the spine-tingling realization surfaced that I had recently read a first-hand account of an eviction on this exact spot, 200 years before.

Mary Cameron describes how her family and neighbours were forced to leave their homes by the 'officers of the law'. In what we would now think of as a post-traumatic memory, she says, 'The hissing of the fire on the flag of the hearth as they were drowning it, reached my heart.' She left, carrying a baby, leading a toddler, and with another child by her side. Her husband carried his infirm mother in a basket. They sat for a while on a hill overlooking the place where they had been brought up, watching as the thatch was torn from the roofs of their houses or set alight. The family seemed in shock: tears would come only later. 'On the day of our leaving Unnimore I thought my heart would rend. I would feel right if my tears would flow; but no relief thus did I find.'[7]

McIntosh names his sadness for lost ways of life using the Gaelic term *cianalas*, which he describes variously as melancholy, a gnawing burden, soul-felt wearisomeness, and a wistful longing. In the context of the Clearances and economic migration, it denotes a longing for home felt by those exiled from the traditional Gaelic-speaking communities of the Highlands and islands. A similar term is the Welsh *hiraeth*, which has cognate words in Cornish and Breton. Across the Celtic fringe, it seems, there has been a need to express a keen sense of anguished yearning, rooted in dislocation from land, community, language and culture.

Wry nostalgia

Yet the past is never as simple as nostalgia would make out. Another face of nostalgia rejects the nostalgic idealization of the past, insisting on a wry realism that is, nevertheless, still filled with longing. Alasdair MacLean's *Night Falls on Ardnamurchan* is a lyrical, but realistic, account of the 'twilight of a crofting family'. His observations begin from his father's terse diaries and widen out to describe the whole crofting enterprise: an Eden in miniature of evening ceilidhs and home-made bannocks; and an underworld of poverty, uncertainty and things never quite working out the way you had hoped. He witnesses both visions of community vanish. His 'twilight' aches with loss, at the same time as recognizing that crofting was a way of life that was always marginal: as units of self-sufficiency, they had been designed to fail. After the Clearances, evicting landlords believed they could not allow people to become too comfortable in their new homes; they needed hungry labourers who would commit to the burgeoning fishing industry along their shores.⁸ The litany of abuses suffered by crofters continued through the nineteenth century, and was not heard until the Napier Commission in the 1880s. It is no wonder that the depopulation of the Highlands evokes powerful emotions: anger, loss and the anguished yearning for home that is *cianalas* and *nostos-algos*. Wry nostalgia refuses to rose-wash past injustices.

Still, our nostalgia for the bounded community persists, as if we were trying to return to the womb. Islands seem particularly prone to this nostalgic idealization. Their fixed boundaries seem to promise a discrete group of people, bonded closely in ties of culture, language and community. Yet, as Alasdair MacLean's *Night Falls on Ardnamurchan* demonstrates, the reality of small communities in a remote rural setting was always more complicated than the aspirational lifestyle magazines would have you believe. MacLean (who regarded Ardnamurchan as an island) and his father used to escape through the back of the house when they saw a certain neighbour coming, with shortcake, to visit (*ceilidh*) for the evening, leaving his mother to welcome the visitor. Human nature is not purified by the air; nor are islands populated by saints or heroes, but by real human beings. Tamsin Calidas shatters the myth of the romantic island getaway in her account of her flight from her graffitied home in London to live off-grid in Argyll. Although she proved to be a resourceful crofter, her experience on an island was of cruelty, misogyny, intimidation and racism, with some innocent bystanders seemingly unable to help.⁹ Nostalgic enchantment can come to an end in realism and disenchantment.

Vicarious nostalgia

Another face of nostalgia attaches not to our own losses but to the losses of others. It seems nostalgia can be felt vicariously. I have never been evicted from my home by a rapacious landlord; yet I can weep at the sight of a clearance village, as if it were once my own home. Richard Holloway, in his account of growing up in the industrial town of Alexandria in West Dunbartonshire recalls how such vicarious nostalgia was expressed in the fireside songs of his youth. Even as a boy, he remembered being puzzled at the adults' deeply felt emotions as his mother sang an emigrant's lament.

> And there wouldn't be a dry eye in the room. It was a strange thing, missing Scotland when we were right there in the middle of it, being overwhelmed with homesickness when we were sitting in our own kitchen before a blazing fire.[10]

Many a fireside song has rehearsed the pain of eviction and emigration – the bleak disaster of Culloden and the outrage of Glencoe – sung by people remote from these events. As a boy, I remember learning 'The Skye Boat Song' in school music lessons, tears pricking my eyes. Even today, in the stands of Murrayfield, the song of a 700-year-old battle can cause rugby supporters to weep, and not only at the prospect of the final score. Vicarious nostalgia suggests that something more than simple homesickness or patriotic feeling is at work here. It is as if our own unnamed losses have become entangled in a cultural memory; and their recovery is bound up with the attempt to return to an idealized past or an earthly paradise.

Yet, despite all this, we continue to believe. We project our own losses and longings onto an idealized period or place and go in search of it to attempt to recover what we have lost. I think of a widow who returned, year after year, to a favourite holiday spot to recreate photos she had taken of herself and her husband while he was still alive. Special memories can seem like a fairytale. It was as if she needed to reassure herself that their life together had really existed; and perhaps a part of her was hoping that one day he would reappear in the frame, filling the empty space.

Ultimate nostalgia

One final face: perhaps nowhere is the wistful longing of nostalgia to be found more than in the contemplation of death – nostalgia as the longing for an ultimate home. In Celtic mythology, the object of this longing is located in the west, the place where the setting sun dips below the horizon: the paradise of *Tìr nan Òg*, the Land of the Young. Perhaps because of the sun's trajectory, the west has been associated with our final resting place. Ian Bradley notes that nearly all the coffin roads in the West Highlands run from east to west.[11] These roads are the traditional routes along which the coffins of the deceased were carried on their final journey, to be buried in a place of spiritual significance. Richard Mabey observes that, in parts of East Anglia, 'the grain of the old landscape – trackways, field boundaries, even the edges of woods – [is] unmistakably tilted towards the west'.[12] Henry Thoreau believed that 'westing' was a basic instinct in living things: 'Eastward I go only by force; but westward I go free.'[13] It is as if humans cannot help but veer towards the setting summer sun.

Others will feel differently, no doubt. We are not all equally 'nostalgia prone'. The degree to which we feel nostalgia may be correlated to traits such as empathy or to our attachment style, for example.[14] Yet I suspect that in most of us, to a greater or lesser extent, there are deep sorrows and longings that attach to a period or a place. This raises the question of the meaning of this experience. If nostalgia is more than homesickness, what is it that we long for? If the paradise island is a mirage, what is the thing we are really seeking after?

The spirituality of nostalgia

There are different answers to this question, depending on the kind of loss to which nostalgia points. At the simplest level, nostalgia may offer an escape from the feeling that our life has become routine, frenetic or meaningless. As we have seen, we wonder if there may be greener grass over a horizon or in the recovery of a simpler past. We project our hoped-for fantasies onto islands or the countryside; or we seek out new relationships or a career change. At a collective level, populist nationalism often feeds on contemporary discontents and looks for an escape to an imagined past when, say, Britain and America were once truly 'great'. The honeymoon period rarely lasts, however, as we cannot sustain an idealized view of our new partner, job or neighbours. Sooner or later, we are faced with the reality of fallible humans or routine work; and most of all, ourselves. What promised to be an escape turns out to be little more than a change of backdrop to the repeating drama of our inner worlds.

Stability

The monastic tradition understands this human restlessness. In his sixth-century monastic *Rule*, St Benedict laid out three monastic vows: not the familiar vows of poverty, chastity and obedience that belonged to the later Franciscan orders, but vows of obedience, the common life (*conversatio morum*) and *stability*. Benedict was critical of itinerant monks, whom he described as 'restless, servants to the seduction of their own will and appetites'.[15]

The latter vow, stability, means staying put, especially remaining in the community in which you find yourself. As Father Christopher Jamison writes, 'For Benedict, simply staying the course with other people is a vital step in spiritual living and hence the vow of stability, the vow to join a specific community for life.'[16] Benedict recognized that the hardest part of monastic life was not frugality or prayer, but simply getting on with others. Living in community has always been challenging; its difficulty might make some lost aspect of our former life all the more attractive and leave us pining for what we once had. The vow of stability is a kind of formalized invitation to stay with your discomfort with the present and seek to find contentment in the everyday.

This invitation can be widened: we may not be monks but the people and routines in our daily lives are likely to chafe and strain at us nevertheless. Like boats tethered to the harbour wall, it can seem as if we are checked in our wandering by a frayed but unyielding rope. We may be safe in harbour, but it doesn't feel like it. We long to take to the open sea, to go in search of contentment and security in some other home. The ancient wisdom of the vow of stability invites us to take a second look at what lies around us. Is the harbour so bad? How much of the restlessness I feel in this crowded space is down to the jostling of my neighbours? How much lies within me? The invitation to stability need not always be about staying put or remaining with difficult people. (Indeed, in some situations, it may be important to leave.) But it is an invitation to examine our inner discontentment to know ourselves better. If spirituality is about connection and insight, then the path of spiritual maturity must surely pass the door of an honest appraisal of our inner restlessness. What is it I am really being drawn to, deep down? Nostalgia can function as escapism: like entering a dark cinema on a bright Saturday afternoon. It can be entertainment. But its risk is in leading us further away from ourselves, as we try to recover some part of us that has been lost. If we locate the lost self in a pot at the end of the rainbow, we will be a long time finding it. Benedictine stability invites us to find ourselves, and our own contentment, in the here and now.

Tending ourselves

The idea of stability can sound somewhat austere: a kind of spiritual, like-it-or-lump-it directive. Yet the process of self-reflection that comes from the initial resolve to stay with our sense of discontent can be an opportunity for self-compassion. The losses and longings of our own nostalgic dreams can be seen as signposts pointing to the fact that something within us needs tending.

When we idealize a person, place or past event – for example, when we fall in love – one way of understanding this is that we have discovered, in the other, a lost or denied part of our own selves. Unconsciously, we see in them the thing we have lost, and the powerful attraction we feel can be an attempt to recover it. Idealizations, such as those concerning romance or nostalgia, can, therefore, provide important clues to the parts of us that are somehow missing: the fun-loving woman, who was brought up in a limiting and rule-bound family, finds herself unusually attracted to inconsistent and risk-taking men. The man, who was raised believing his talent for drawing was worthless, ends up with a partner who is a visual artist. In the case of nostalgia, it may be that we have actively projected some part of ourselves onto a place or a past event in the hope of recovering it. The question we might then ask is, 'What does this nostalgia point to *in me*? What *in me* needs tending? Is there a lost part of me that is asking to be recovered or, perhaps, mourned?'

Understood in this way, we might discover that our nostalgias are really nostalgia for our truer selves, which over time have been forgotten – or overridden; perhaps they lie hidden under layers of shame.

For a long time, I had a recurring dream. In it, I am in a huge, rambling house with many storeys and many rooms. Wandering the upper corridors, I find a small door in a wall, just big enough to crawl through. Behind the door there is a tiny stair. I crawl up it to the floor above. There is a locked door, but I find a key that lets me in. The room is light and airy. There is a desk and a computer, with an ongoing project under way – something I half-remember starting. No one knows this room is here. I have a dim feeling that I recognize this place, and I am filled with wonder.

I long to get back to that room. But where is it? I suspect it is within me. It is where the spontaneous part of me might be now, were it not constrained by layers of expectation and shame that I have internalized over the years. Gerard Manley Hopkins speaks powerfully of this condition in his poem 'As Kingfishers Catch Fire'. He is informed by the Ignatian insight that there is a unique, divinely made core to each of us, and that spiritual maturity involves paying heed to its call and consolation. In the poem, he praises creatures that act from their very being:

> As kingfishers catch fire, dragonflies draw flame ...
> Stones ring; like each tucked string tells, each hung bell's
> Bow swung finds tongue to fling out broad its name.

Each of these, he says,

> goes itself; *myself* it speaks and spells,
> Crying *Whát I dó is me: for that I came.*
> (Gerard Manley Hopkins, 'As Kingfishers Catch Fire')[17]

Nostalgia invites us to look within at our own losses, and to wonder what it is that we long to recover. In the spontaneity of a child playing, we can see most clearly the beauty of 'what I do is me'. Perhaps we can wonder at what it would be like to return to this place in ourselves. This might begin from noticing 'what I do' when the constraints are off – a creative project, a cranky thought, a spontaneous gesture. It may be a not-so-nice aspect of ourselves. So be it. If we can acknowledge and welcome our whole selves, our response to this can also become part of 'what I do is me'.

The search for home

'Oh yes, it's "just" nostalgia,' wrote McIntosh, at the sight of the rotting boat. His wry minimizing of his experience hints at the possibility that there could be more to nostalgia than mere lachrymose sentimentality. Indeed, for McIntosh, nostalgia 'opens up a deeper way of seeing'. Our idealistic longings may be clues that we need to attend to our inner worlds before we run for the hills. But they may also be signposts of a different sort.

There is a long tradition of thought that sees the restless heart as a signpost to the place of true rest. Perhaps the best-known formulation of this is in St Augustine's prayer. Observing that God has 'stirred him up', he prays, 'Thou has created us for thyself, and our heart knows no rest until it may repose in thee.'[18]

Far from seeing nostalgia as escapism, this approach invites us to take our desires seriously as signposts to transcendent objects. On this view, our *nostos-algos* – our anguished longing for home – is transposed to a spiritual plane. Our yearning for 'home' is a longing for a place of eternal rest, a desire with no earthly fulfilment. Restlessness seems built into the human condition. The ancient wisdom of Ecclesiastes tells us that '[God] has ... set eternity in the human heart' (Ecc. 3.11, NIV).

C. S. Lewis articulated this experience of a desire that points beyond any earthly fulfilment in a sensation he termed 'joy'. He describes this as 'an unsatisfied desire that is itself more desirable than any other satisfaction'.[19] In his early life he became aware of 'sickeningly intense' experiences of wonder: the 'Idea of Autumn'; the 'cool, dewy, fresh, exuberant' properties of a garden; or the 'huge regions of northern sky' encountered while reading a Norse saga. For Lewis, joy is not simple happiness or pleasure. 'It must have the stab, the pang, the inconsolable longing.' Like nostalgia, 'it might almost equally well be called a particular kind of unhappiness or grief'.[20]

Sometimes we misread the signpost. One way of understanding our British obsession with home ownership is to see it as a proxy for the spiritual quest. The language we use is revealing.

We look for our 'ideal home', our 'dream home', our 'forever home'. Tim Gorringe notes that North American developers never build 'houses' but 'homes': 'a word that, as John Steinbeck observed, reduces Americans to tears'.[21] The desire for a safe, dependable home is understandable. Yet our yearning for a 'dream' home may partly be a symbol of our longing for a place of ultimate rest.

The anguished longing for an ultimate home may also be a spiritual response to our existential condition, as creatures trapped within the relentless sequence of time. As the mindfulness guru Jon Kabat-Zinn puts it, we live our lives 'in the only moment we ever get, which is this one'.[22] We seem to pass through time but never occupy it. We are so habituated to this movement, that we cease to wonder at it. Mindfulness is one attempt to 'occupy' the present by being present to ourselves. We also strive to create a liveable space on the razor-edge of the present by borrowing from the past and the future; we reminisce and anticipate; perhaps we return to the same place on holiday, year after year, to reassure ourselves that we can recycle the present moment and revisit it again. 'So many summers,' wrote MacCaig, 'and I have lived them too.'

I wonder if nostalgia is another way in which we quell this existential anxiety. The relentless sequence of time not only keeps us on a treadmill, but it also points us forward to the moment when our time will run out. As we age, we may become increasingly conscious that each summer we live through is being spent from a diminishing and finite store of summers. There is some evidence that nostalgia supports the psychological well-being of older people, as they face up to limited time horizons.[23] Harvesting the satisfactions of memory may be one aspect of this. It may also be that the wistful longing for 'home' alerts us to our deeper desire for a place of eternal 'rest'. Nostalgia awakens in us a sense of transcendence. It enables us to place our frenetic moments, and diminishing years, in the wider context of eternity; perhaps, to rest in the arms of the 'Father of the heavenly lights, who does not change like shifting shadows' (James 1.17, NIV).

Nostalgia, then, is a particular kind of grief. It is a wistful longing or anguished yearning for an unrecoverable place or past. It may point to neglected parts of ourselves and invite us to befriend these as an alternative to pursuing an escapist fantasy. It may offer clues to areas of our inner lives that lie untended, and that may be clamouring to be acknowledged or even mourned. Equally, nostalgia may be a holy discontent, pointing us beyond our visible horizon to the fulfilment of our deepest spiritual longings.

Notes

1 Norman MacCaig, 2011, 'So Many Summers', in *The Poems of Norman MacCaig*, Edinburgh: Polygon, p. 216. Reproduced with permission of the Licensor through PLSclear.

2 A. McIntosh, 2023, *Poacher's Pilgrimage*, 2nd ed., Edinburgh: Birlinn Ltd, p. 79.

3 J. Rebanks, 2020, *English Pastoral*, London: Allen Lane, p. 15.

4 H. Ritchie, M. Roser and V. Samborska, 2018, 'Urbanization', Our World in Data (revised Dec. 2024), at https://ourworldindata.org/urbanization, accessed 14.04.2025.

5 McIntosh, *Poacher's Pilgrimage*, p. 200.

6 Inniemore is an anglicized version of the Gaelic name of the adjacent mountain.

7 N. Macleod, 2002, *Morvern: A Highland parish*, Edinburgh: Birlinn Ltd, pp. 178–9.

8 D. P. Willis, 1991, *The Story of Crofting in Scotland*, Edinburgh: John Donald. Patrick Sellar, the factor of the Duke of Sutherland, who instigated the notorious clearances in Strathnaver, described the estate policy as one where coastal land should be allocated 'in lots under the size of three arable acres, sufficient for the maintenance of an industrious family, but pinched enough to cause them to turn their attention to fishing' (pp. 37–8).

9 T. Calidas, 2020, *I Am an Island*, London: Doubleday.

10 R. Holloway, 2012, *Leaving Alexandria: A memoir of faith and doubt*, Edinburgh: Canongate Books, p. 30.

11 I. Bradley, 2022, *The Coffin Roads*, Edinburgh: Birlinn Ltd.

12 R. Mabey, 2008, *Nature Cure*, London: Vintage Books, p. 81.

13 H. D. Thoreau, 'Walking', *The Atlantic Monthly*, 9/56 (1862), pp. 657–74, p. 662.

14 J. Juhl, T. Wildschut, C. Sedikides, T. Diebel, W. Cheung and A.

J. J. M. Vingerhoets, 'Nostalgia Proneness and Empathy: Generality, underlying mechanism, and implications for prosocial behavior', *Journal of Personality*, 88/3 (2019), pp. 485–500, at https://doi.org/10.1111/jopy.12505, accessed 14.04.2025.

15 A. C. Meisel and M. L. del Mastro (eds), 2010, *The Rule of St. Benedict*, New York, NY: Image, p. 47.

16 C. Jamison, 2006, *Finding Sanctuary: Monastic steps for everyday life*, London: Weidenfeld & Nicolson, p. 118.

17 Gerard Manley Hopkins, 2009, 'Kingfisher', in Catherine Phillips (ed.), *Gerard Manley Hopkins: The major works*, Oxford: Oxford University Press.

18 R. Hudleston (ed.), 1963, *The Confessions of St Augustine*, trans. T. Matthew, London: Fontana, p. 31.

19 C. S. Lewis, 1959, *Surprised by Joy*, London: Fontana, p. 20. Lewis's somewhat peculiar choice of the word 'joy' to describe this experience may have been down to his relationship with Joy Davidman, which was developing around the time of writing. Lewis was indeed 'surprised by joy', which is a quote from Wordsworth and the title of Lewis's autobiography.

20 Lewis, *Surprised by Joy*, p. 62.

21 T. Gorringe, 2002, *A Theology of the Built Environment*, Cambridge: Cambridge University Press, p. 80.

22 Quoted in M. Williams and D. Penman, 2011, *Mindfulness: A practical guide to finding peace in a frantic world*, London: Piatkus, p. ix.

23 N. J. Kelley, W. E. Davis, J. Dang, L. Liu, T. Wildschut and C. Sedikides, 'Nostalgia Confers Psychological Wellbeing by Increasing Authenticity', *Journal of Experimental Social Psychology*, 102 (2022), pp. 1–12, at https://www.sciencedirect.com/science/article/pii/S0022103122000981?via%3Dihub, accessed 14.04.2025.

6

Failure

Worse than failure, perhaps, is feeling trapped inside a cycle of overachievement in pursuit of a success that at heart you don't believe in. (Joe Moran, *If You Should Fail*)[1]

Another loss we are bound to encounter – in some form or other – is the experience of failure. Big or small, failure can be painful and filled with shame. We're dropped from the sports team; our job application is rejected; our business goes under. Perhaps we've been told we're 'good for nothing'. *Failure*, in the music of the word itself, is set in a minor key, in stark contrast to its bouncy counterpart, *success*, which seems to burst from the wings with jazz hands and a crazy grin. Success! Ta-da! As we shall see, these binary options have not always existed; but it may help us to know failure better by beginning with success. What do our typical notions of success look like?

King Harry the Ninth

At the centre of St Andrew's Square in Edinburgh's New Town stands a fluted stone column, towering 150 feet over an oval pattern of lawns and pathways below. Perched on top is a statue of Henry Dundas, Lord Melville, 15 feet tall and weighing 18 tons. Dundas was the pre-eminent statesman in Scotland in the second half of the eighteenth century. Such was his power that he became known colloquially as 'King Harry the Ninth', which was only half in jest as, at the time of his death in 1811, no British monarch had set foot in Scotland for 160 years. Although lacking noble birth, his brilliant legal mind, political astuteness and soaring ambition saw him rise unchallenged to power. Born in 1742, he was Solicitor General for Scotland by the age of 24; by the time he was 33, he was Lord Advocate. In his late 30s, he became the sole Keeper of the Signet: a role that gave him pre-eminent control over appointments to government posts in Scotland. He was able to use his position to establish a following of 'clients, voters and local interests, who depended on [him] for favours, places, promotions and pensions'.[2] From 1790, he was elected Member of Parliament for Edinburgh; he served as Home Secretary, President of the Board of Control, and Secretary of State for War. In that same election year, he personally controlled 34 of the 41 Scottish constituencies. His close relationship with the younger William Pitt was cemented by royal drinking sessions and Pitt's dependence on him to maintain support in Scotland.

In death, as in life, Dundas's supremacy over Scotland was assured. At one time, a plan was mooted to build a memorial pyramid to him on the capital's highest hill, Arthur's Seat.[3] The actual monument built in St Andrew's Square was based on Trajan's column in Rome. Dundas was not a pharaoh, but perhaps he could be remembered as an emperor. Whether intended or not, his great statue stands with its back to the Georgian mansion of his *nouveau-riche* rival, Lawrence Dundas, and looks down the spine of the New Town upon the head of the diminutive figure of George IV.

For nearly two hundred years, Dundas's legacy went largely unchallenged; the spare assessment on his memorial plaque read, 'A dominant figure in politics for over four decades.' More recently, his reputation has come under scrutiny as his relationship to the slave trade has been investigated. The City Council and Dundas's descendants and supporters have tussled over the wording of a revisionist plaque at the base of his column that reads, 'Dedicated to the memory of more than half-a-million Africans whose enslavement was a consequence of Henry Dundas's actions.'

Wherever we stand on this debate, Dundas has stood for two centuries as a symbol of success: rising to power, wealth, influence and high office in the state; a man held up before the eyes of his nation as a towering figure who still towers over Scotland's capital. No doubt our questions about his role in the slave trade are important, but there's something else here that demands revision: our model of success.

The archetype of the 'great white man' atop a sandstone pillar still lurks in our psyches and dogs our dreams. Our goals may have moved since the eighteenth century, but perhaps not far: fame, wealth, influence and reputation remain our criteria for success. We swoon before celebrities, and marvel at the achievements of global entrepreneurs, elite athletes and fearless explorers. Our pedestals may no longer be made of stone, but we build them nevertheless: from the plywood rostrum by the athletics track to the nine-figure platform of social-media followers, accrued by some global celebrities. In the absence of these, we often apply a still cruder metric to measure the success of our fellow humans – so-called 'net worth'. As the US bumper-sticker puts it, only half in jest, 'He who dies with the most toys wins.'

Ironically, Dundas would not have been called a 'success' in his lifetime. This use of the word is more recent. Our first examples of 'success' used to describe 'a thing or person that succeeds' is from 1882. Likewise, 'failure', meaning an identity rather than an incident, only appeared in the US in 1865.[4] Yet these Victorian inventions followed from the Enlightenment's unshakeable belief that humanity was progressing in every department of human life, from technology to welfare, education to science. Perhaps this seems self-evident to us now and we no longer question it; but, stepping back, we might discern that splicing human endeavour into categories of 'success' and 'failure' is an ideological move. We apply them to exams, job interviews, marriages, careers, businesses, and even to our felt sense of who we are. The relatively recent coining of the terms tells us something: it was not always thus.

ALL IS NOT LOSS

The success of success

How did success come to have such currency? Until recently many schoolchildren would have been familiar with the Victorian jingle, 'If at first you don't succeed, try, try again.' It appears as a line in a three-verse hymn to perseverance, in T. H. Palmer's *The Teacher's Manual*, published in Boston in 1840. Significantly, it is presented in a chapter on 'Moral Education', framing perseverance as a *moral* virtue. He lists perseverance in a table of 57 virtues, a Heinz-like inventory, together 'with their opposite vices'. If perseverance is a virtue, it follows in Palmer's scheme that 'irresolution and instability' are vices. From here, it's a short step to seeing ultimate success as a virtue and failure as a moral flaw. The implication seems clear: 'If in the end you don't succeed, you weren't trying hard enough.' If success belongs to the virtuous and the industrious, then failure is freighted with shame.

The moral prestige of success, then, carries a devastating counterpart: the ignominy of failure. When we moralize the binary options of success and failure, we set ourselves up for a new species of pain and loss. Believing we have failed at something can undermine our sense of our abilities and worth. It can be a source of acute shame: one of the most painful emotions, as shame often rests on a fear of losing others' love. Failure can undermine our social status, leave us poorer, and dash our hopes and dreams. It can leach opportunity. Over time, it can gnaw holes in our self-esteem and cause us to tell ourselves doleful stories about who we really are and how others must see us. As failures congeal into an identity – *feeling* a failure – we can come to believe that this is just the way we are. It can be hard to see or acknowledge that failure is a loss, let alone allow ourselves the space to grieve it.

The success of success, then, has cast a deep shadow over failure; so much so that we struggle to accept failure or allow that it could be a normal part of everyday life.

The myth of redemptive failure

In western culture, the denial of failure has become something of an industry. In the 1990s, the film *Apollo 13* popularized the phrase 'failure is not an option'. When the lives of three astronauts were in jeopardy, failure was indeed unthinkable. Since then, however, the phrase has entered the language of motivational speakers and the business world. It has become a mode of denial, an incantation trusted to ward off the spectre of failure by the force of mere repetition.

Following the dot-com crash of 2000, failure became harder to brush aside; a new emphasis emerged on 'failing well'. Failure was reframed as redemptive. A rash of books appeared, with titles such as *Adapt: Why success always starts with failure*; *Fail Fast, Fail Often: How losing can help you win*; or *The Up Side of Down: Why failing well is the key to success*. In this world, failure is never mere failure, but a stepping-stone to success.

Of course, there is some truth here. Success may come on the back of failed attempts; and, as the writer Frank Cottrell Boyce has suggested, failure can be 'success in waiting' or 'the loam on which ideas are born'.[5] Apart from errors that prove fatal, we can usually learn from our mistakes. Yet there is a danger that all failure comes to be interpreted in this way: something that Joe Moran describes as 'looking at failure through the rear-view mirror of the successful'.[6] He highlights how the 'tote-bag-friendly'[7] 'Fail Better' slogan has become an inspirational quote, the very opposite of what was meant by its gloomy author, Samuel Beckett, who simply meant 'plod on'. Moran reminds us that not all failure is productive. There is such a thing as abject failure; the notion that failure is always redemptive is a myth.

A spirituality of failure will begin where spirituality must always begin – with things as they are, not as we would hope or pretend them to be. No doubt there are moments when failure can be 'leveraged' to hoist us skywards into the realms of success. But what interests me here is our experience of *abject* failure – failure that comes with no redemptive arc – and the losses that this entails. Only by acknowledging the loss that is failure can we properly begin to grieve it; and it is only in the honesty of grieving that we can begin to listen for what spiritual invitation it may cradle. If, as Moran suggests, 'failure is the small print in the terms and conditions of being human',[8] then failure seems to be common and universal. How, then, might its still, small voice speak?

The spirituality of failure

In previous chapters, we have seen some of the ways in which the grief from loss might carry an invitation to spiritual connection, insight and growth. When we have failed, abjectly and irrevocably, is there anything we can recover? Sitting among the smouldering ashes of the people and projects that once held our hearts, is it any help to wonder if, perhaps, 'all is not loss'? If failure is mostly 'just a waste of time',[9] should we risk any more time in listening for its invitation?

This is not inevitable or guaranteed; but when a type of loss is pervasive and universal, it seems worth asking whether human beings have found their grief to be adaptive in some way. Or, in the language of spirituality, we can ask whether our grief at failing might be fertile soil in which faith, relationships, wisdom and values may grow.

Vulnerability and co-operation

One way the grief of failure might speak to us is in the invitation to co-operate, rather than compete. Success is often competitive. This is appropriate for an athlete; unavoidable in business; and, in life, it is a respectable form of antisocial behaviour by, for example, 'sharp-elbowed' parents, who get their children into the best schools, or 'social climbers', who have learned to turn networking to their advantage.

Yet, there is a paradox to this success. As well as these benefits, we may also want success to give us something that only others can give, namely, approval, adulation, love. 'In search of it, we drive through our lives in little armoured tanks of ego,' Moran suggests. 'Inside these tanks, we try to do two irreconcilable things: compete with others, and win their approval and love.'[10] It is the paradox of the Hollywood acceptance speech that those who win the awards often want to say that the accolade is deserved by almost anyone except themselves. This may be humility; but I also wonder whether we shrink from the solitary confinement of the pedestal or rostrum because we fear losing others' love. Perhaps we anticipate envious attack. We long to say that, despite our success, we are still 'one of you'. We deflect the adulation, while craving the attention success brings. 'Humbled to have been awarded ...' begins the so-called 'humble-bragging' of many a social-media post.

It's lonely at the top

Dundas cuts a lonely figure on top of his pale, fluted column. There is no one up there with him to share the view. If his column is a metaphor for success, it reminds us that it's lonely at the top. And even if he enjoyed the adulation of much of Britain in his lifetime, two centuries later his star has fallen, and his column has become a pillar of shame. Success is lonely and fragile; it is also mean. It defines the narrow plinth on which our lives are made to count for something; it ignores the lush undergrowth of possibility in which every life could flourish.

Failure is not the opposite of success but its misnamed alternative. In bright weather, the square beneath Dundas's column is typically strewn with tourists sipping coffee, or groups of students playing acoustic instruments on the lush grass or stretching out beneath the trees. If competitive success divides us, failure can bring us together. Indeed, it is the vulnerability we experience when we have failed that can be the very thing that enables others to reach out to us. In the absence of vulnerability, we are hard to reach in our 'little armoured tanks of ego'. Failure places us in love's way or, as the contemplative nun Maria Boulding put it, 'If we cannot endure failing and being weak ... we are not yet in a position to love and be loved.'[11] Failure can also be the gateway to laughter and self-acceptance,[12] a homely atmosphere where, in Beckett's words, we may breathe 'deep of its vivifying air'.[13]

High expectations

If we have lived with high expectations, we may find it hard to believe that failure could open us to love and laughter. If we fail in our exams or our career, how will we face those who may have sacrificed their own comfort to bring us opportunity. We may also have internalized those high expectations, so that we can't imagine how we will live with *ourselves* if we don't succeed.

For some, the sense of unrealistic goals set for us by our ambitious parents is transferred to God, whom we experience as a hard task master and an unremitting perfectionist. Under these circumstances, it can feel, absolutely, as if 'failure is not an option'. The reality of failure can seem like an existential threat. The public shame and personal loathing (not to mention an angry god) become too much to face.

In November 2022, Caversham Primary School underwent a statutory Office for Standards in Education (Ofsted) inspection, which downgraded the school's rating from 'outstanding' to 'inadequate' on the basis that it failed on the one criterion of safeguarding. The head teacher, Ruth Perry, who had been in post for 13 years, ended her life by suicide in January 2023, while waiting for the full report. An inquest found that she had no relevant mental health history. We can never know exactly what leads a person to end their life, yet we do know here what preceded it: the replacement of a single word. Suicide is often a response to feeling trapped; it may have seemed to Ruth Perry that there was no way back from this four-syllable judgement.

This is a tragic example, but many of us will have felt the pain of something similar. We may not plan to end our lives, but failure may cause us to feel as if our lives have ended. The 'failed' business, career, pregnancy or relationship – whatever counts as failure in our experience – is a loss that needs to be acknowledged and mourned before we can begin to hear the quiet invitation of grief. It may be months or years before we can discern this voice amid our tears. Yet, giving up the hope of climbing the pedestal of our own expectations can open us up to alternatives. Allowing ourselves to be vulnerable can allow others to come alongside. We can find new ways to flourish that are more life-affirming than the scripts we inherited and internalized. Success can be redefined: it can become less about *me* and more about *us*. The invitation of grief may whisper to us that failure *is* an option, after all.

Reframing failure

A few years ago, I left my job as the rector of a small Anglican church and embarked on a life as a freelance journalist. In the weeks leading up to my leaving, I had a dream that I was on board a ship. Life on the ship had become unbearable; the only way out for me was to 'walk the plank'. Blindfolded, I stepped forward, not knowing whether the ship was in harbour or sailing on a vast, empty ocean.

I left my secure job with little more than the birthday money from my parents in my back pocket, no savings, and three children to support. Still, leaving felt safer than staying. I had reached a vocational impasse; the career I had signed up for was leaving me too anxious to function and I didn't know why. I was proud of my courage and energized by the tasks of writing and producing small films, even if the freelance life was somewhat hand-to-mouth.

A year or two passed, and I realized there were still some warm vocational embers from my previous life. I began to explore a new direction, in the form of health-care chaplaincy.

I spoke to people. I read a lot. I applied for jobs. I hoped that my 20 years in pastoral ministry and a doctoral degree in the sociology of religion might count for something. But as the job rejections mounted up, I felt as if they might be doing the opposite. Rejection can feel quite personal.

Jobs were few and far between; I often spent months watching empty spaces on recruitment websites. One day, I found myself preparing for my twelfth job interview. More than ever, it seemed as if this was make or break. I *had* to succeed or face a frightening and unknown consequence. In the midst of this hailstorm of anxiety, I stumbled on shelter: the sudden realization that *failure is an option*. I googled the phrase, found a T-shirt emblazoned with this slogan and clicked 'add to cart'. Staring at the rich hinterland of failure became an important part of my preparation.

I'm almost sorry to say, I got the job. The T-shirt still lies, unbought, in a virtual shopping cart somewhere: I will never know where else it might have taken me. I don't wish to minimize the anguish, grief and despair another rejection would have meant. But, even in the midst of such a loss, I might have glimpsed something beyond; as the Quaker writer Jennifer Kavanagh puts it: 'It is at times of failure and brokenness that we become able to see another dimension, open ourselves up to faith.'[14] Of course, that's easy for me to say: I got the job in the end. Perhaps I'm sailing close to 'looking at failure through the rear-view mirror of the successful'. But then, I haven't told you my whole story.

Recalibrating expectations

Failure is indeed an option. The grief of failing invites us to see things differently. Failure often rides on a set of expectations – criteria for what counts as success – that are driven by cultural norms, reinforced by our family of origin and internalized by ourselves. In this sense, we literally set ourselves up for failure. Mostly, these expectations serve us well. They may drive us to fulfil our potential, contribute to society and reap certain rewards.

But, as we have seen, when we fail, these criteria can come to haunt us. The yardstick we have been using to measure success will also define our failure. For the perfectionist, almost everything will seem like failure. But even for those for whom 'good enough is good enough', a nagging inner voice can leave them 'never feeling good enough'. The balance seems tipped against us. Success, when it comes, can feel external and temporary, whereas failure 'digs deep into the human psyche'.[15]

But what if we were to recalibrate our expectations? Failure may whisper that the time has come to revise them. Perhaps they were never *our* expectations in the first place, but the anxious hopes of parents or teachers. Maybe we were thrown into a competition we never wanted to win. Perhaps we are coming to the conclusion that life does not consist of beating the opposition. Failing may cause us to look again at the rules of the game and wonder why we set out to play that particular game in the first place.

We don't have to play the game, whichever game it is that tells us we have failed. Failure is an option because, beyond the rostrum, there may be a level field on which the many can flourish, in their own way, not just the few. And if failure feels more spacious than success, it may also feel more familiar. Joe Moran makes the intriguing suggestion that 'failure feels like coming home'. In an echo of the Last Supper, failure 'is where we meet and break bread with other weak and wavering mortals'. Perhaps this explains why we can feel nostalgic about our failures: the pressure is off, our slippers are on and we are home. Only there can we 'live life in all its fullness and fecundity'.[16]

The view from the ash heap

The ultimate riches to rags story is found in one of the oldest books of the Hebrew Bible, the Book of Job. Job was a successful man, 'the greatest man among all the people of the East' (Job 1.3, NIV). But soon disaster comes to him: all his wealth, in the form of his animals, is stolen. His servants are killed. His children die in a storm. His skin breaks out in painful sores. By the end of the second chapter, we find him deep in grief, sitting on a heap of ashes, scraping his sores with a shard of broken pottery. There he sits for the next 40 chapters, protesting his innocence and batting away the insensitive theories of his 'comforters', who think they can diagnose his misfortune and prescribe a remedy.

The book belongs to the tradition of Hebrew 'wisdom literature'. This genre of writing is not intended to provide the answers to our existential dilemmas but, instead, sets the *questions* in ways that invite us to think for ourselves. Only from this wrestling does wisdom emerge. The Book of Job asks whether human devotion can ever be unconditional ('Does Job fear God for nothing?' asks The Satan in Job 1.9), and whether suffering is necessarily a 'deal-breaker' for those who seek to keep faith with the God of Israel ('Curse God and die!' urges Job's wife in Job 2.9).

Job's achievement is that he puts up with nearly forty chapters of 'good advice' on top of his grief and somehow manages to stay with the mystery of his suffering. He knows it is not deserved. He knows it makes no sense. And he doesn't believe that God is behind it.

Part of the wisdom of Job is his example of remaining on the ash heap, refusing glib answers, and waiting and listening for the truth to emerge. Failure can feel like this: it can seem an enforced catastrophe in which we are brought low, and even the 'comfort' of friends can sting. Job's example invites us to stay with the grief of our failure and listen for its invitation. Job whispers that we should resist the urge to tidy up our failure, to gloss over it and move on quickly; in other words, we ought not to deny grief altogether. He challenges the temptation to short-circuit our grief by converting it to guilt and beating ourselves up. He invites us not to hide our grief beneath a cover of anger, nor project it outwards in blame at those whose actions seem to have contributed to our state. 'Without an adequate time in the ashes, tending the loss,' writes Francis Weller, 'sorrow mutates into symptoms of depression, anxiety, dullness and despair.'[17]

Recalibrating worth

Another way the grief of failure might bring us to a more wholesome place is in inviting us to reappraise our values.

We have seen how failure can feel personal; how it can 'dig deep into the human psyche'. The ash heap can leave us feeling charred and brittle. One reason for this is that we commonly peg our sense of self-worth to our achievements so that, when we fail, we experience the deflation of our selves. In the most tragic examples, as we have seen, a single word such as 'inadequate' can bring us down. We may know too well the feeling of wounded desolation following an unsuccessful job interview, a social snub or the end of a romantic relationship. Alternatively, it may be the feeling of irrelevance and inadequacy at finding that a treasured project has been shelved by an employer, or that we have been passed over for promotion. Failure has as many faces as there are people, yet its ability to eat into our self-esteem seems to be universal.

Finding ourselves on the ash heap can become an invitation to recalibrate what matters to us. If spirituality is about growing into our true values and casting off the values of the 'false self' that society has encouraged us to wear, failure can gift us a starting point. Failure can invite us to connect with a sense of our intrinsic worth, whether we understand that to be the birthright of all human beings or something given by virtue of being made in the image of God. Failure invites us to dare to believe that our value was never dependent on the projects, promotions and prizes on which we staked so much. It doesn't hang on whether we have a role in life, or whether we are useful or productive. It doesn't even depend on whether people like us or accept us. The grief of failing strips us back to essentials and invites us to find at the core an 'immortal diamond'.[18]

Failure invites suspicion of success – not because we are poor losers or need to call 'sour grapes', but because there is a better alternative: human flourishing. Flourishing doesn't require us to beat the opposition or strain to fulfil the litany of expectations imposed on us by parents, Ofsted, polite society or whoever. It is not measured by rankings, gongs, statistics or 'net worth'. 'Those who flourish rely on a different scale of values than the ordinary arithmetic of failure and success,' writes Moran.[19] Flourishing allows everyone their own criteria for success. Flourishing only asks: what is coming alive within me, within *us*, that I might notice and nurture?

Courting failure

One of the remarkable features of the Gospels is that Jesus seems to make a point of inverting structures of power by siding with the weak in society and, in some instances, courting failure. He thumbs his nose at the strictures of the religious rulers by failing to observe the Sabbath rules. He hangs out with the 'unclean' and the outcasts from Jewish society: prostitutes, tax-collectors, lepers and foreign women. He is no less vulnerable and provocative towards the Roman occupation of his day. He invites arrest by marching on Jerusalem; he fails to arm adequately his followers in Gethsemane (two swords are enough); and, at his trial, he refuses to defend himself to the Roman governor Pilate.

Jesus is not the only religious founder who has subverted worldly models of power and success; but his example of walking to his death is one of the most vivid. He seemingly places weakness and failure at the heart of his project. Faith traditions, including Christianity, can often help to address our failure because they subvert the values of societies based on status and power; they claim that, in spiritual terms, the normal hierarchies are inverted. The Magnificat proclaims that rulers are brought down; the humble are lifted up; the hungry are filled with good things; the rich are sent away empty. As Maria Boulding says, 'God has dealt with our failure by himself becoming a failure in Jesus Christ and so healing it from the inside.'[20] Once we have seen power and success in these terms it becomes hard not to unsee them: the posturing and performances of powerful world leaders or global magnates appear comic and ridiculous against the sober humility of the Suffering Servant.

A quiet invitation

Abject failure hurts: and there is no guarantee of resurrection. Failure is a loss that asks to be grieved. For some failures, grief will take its course and no more can be said. Other failures, however, may conceal a quiet invitation. Failure might make us curious: are there alternative ways of living, based on a different metric? Are there those that are more about co-operation than competition? What if I turned my attention from asking 'How can I succeed?' to 'How can we flourish?' What if we turned the shame of our failure outward and shared our vulnerability with others? Failure *is* an option because we don't have to play by the rules we inherited. Our worth as people can rest on something more substantial than the paper certificate that declares us to be one of life's winners.

I have conducted dozens of funerals, often for people I have never met. It is a privilege to sit with a family while they paint a word picture of their loved one and I scribble down details. I've noted that people hardly talk about the person's career; they never speak of financial success. A military medal or letter from the Queen might get a mention. But mostly, it's their personal qualities that define them in the end. He was a good father; she was a great friend; he was a lovable rogue. With death in our faces, we know what a 'successful' life looks like.

Notes

1 J. Moran, 2021, *If You Should Fail: Why success eludes us and why it doesn't matter*, London: Penguin, p. 61.
2 T. M. Devine, 2016, *Independence or Union*, London: Penguin, p. 52.
3 Historic Environment Scotland, 2024, 'Edinburgh, St Andrew Square, Melville's Monument', Canmore, at https://canmore.org.uk/site/52413/edinburgh-st-andrew-square-melvilles-monument, accessed 14.04.2025.
4 Moran, *If You Should Fail*, p. 26.
5 Quoted in J. Kavanagh, 2012, *The Failure of Success: Redefining what matters*, Alresford: John Hunt Publishing, pp. 56–7.
6 Moran, *If You Should Fail*, p. 11.
7 Moran, *If You Should Fail*, p. 13.
8 Moran, *If You Should Fail*, p. 134.
9 Moran, *If You Should Fail*, p. 14.
10 Moran, *If You Should Fail*, pp. 14–15.
11 M. Boulding, 1985, *Gateway to Hope: An exploration of failure*, London: Fount, p. 12.
12 Kavanagh, *Failure of Success*, pp. 60f.
13 Quoted in Moran, *If You Should Fail*, p. 13.
14 Kavanagh, *Failure of Success*, p. 74.
15 Kavanagh, *Failure of Success*, p. 63.
16 Moran, *If You Should Fail*, p. 154.
17 F. Weller, 2015, *The Wild Edge of Sorrow: Rituals of renewal and the sacred work of grief*, Berkeley, CA: North Atlantic Books, p. 17.
18 The phrase is from the Jesuit poet Gerard Manley Hopkins, who suffered from episodes of deep depression, never saw his poems published in his lifetime and died at the untimely age of 44.
19 Moran, *If You Should Fail*, p. 67.
20 Boulding, *Gateway to Hope*, p. 9.

7

Shame

'Who told you that you were naked?'
(Genesis 3.11, NRSV)

Disenfranchised grief

Grief is painful enough. Yet its wound can hurt even more when the grief itself is cloaked in shame or secrecy. When we fall silent, feeling that the grief is unacceptable or too personal to name. Sometimes we are not quite sure what we have lost; or we are unable to recognize grief for what it is. Grief that hides in the shadows has been termed 'disenfranchised' grief: the grief that dare not speak its name. As Ken Doka defines it: 'Disenfranchised losses are not openly acknowledged, socially sanctioned, or publicly shared.'[1]

Shame

Disenfranchised grief comes in many forms. When relationships have not been openly acknowledged, for example, the bereaved can be left isolated in their grief.

Until recently it was very common for same-sex couples to live together without being out about their sexuality. When one partner died, the other was left to grieve a partner alone, without the social support a straight married couple might have received. Even today, some same-sex couples from particular faith communities or cultural backgrounds prefer to keep quiet about their relationships, for fear of being ostracized. When a partner dies, the practicalities of mourning may be taken over by the deceased person's birth family, leaving the partner excluded from the funeral or wake. Even when a relationship is public, the bereaved same-sex partner may experience, from others, a subtle disregard of their position as spouse or partner; they may find that they are not offered the empathy that is typically extended to straight bereaved partners. One survey found that almost a quarter of lesbian, gay or bisexual adults expected to face barriers, on account of their sexual identity, when they came to plan a funeral.[2]

In disenfranchised grief, love may be linked to shame. Lord Alfred Douglas's poem 'Two Loves' pictures two men 'walking on a shining plain'. One 'sang of pretty maids / And joyous love of comely girl and boy'. The narrator asks the other his name, and he answers: 'My name is Love.'

> Then straight the first did turn himself to me
> And cried, 'He lieth, for his name is Shame,
> But I am Love, and I was wont to be
> Alone in this fair garden, till he came
> Unasked by night; I am true Love, I fill
> The hearts of boy and girl with mutual flame.'
> Then sighing, said the other, 'Have thy will,
> I am the love that dare not speak its name.'
> (Lord Alfred Douglas, 'Two Loves')[3]

The poem captures the poignancy of a love that has been labelled 'Shame'; a love that 'dare not speak its name'. When this love is ruptured by death, or some other loss, it becomes a *grief* that dare not speak its name. It becomes the disenfranchised grief of a bereaved same-sex partner or, indeed, one of the many forms of disenfranchised loss where shame abounds.

Catherine became pregnant in the early 1960s. She was working in Italy as an au pair after leaving school and fell in love with an artist she met in Florence. When he learned of the pregnancy, he left her. She returned to England, where her parents sent her to a Roman Catholic home for unmarried mothers in Liverpool. There she remained, hidden from view, until the baby was born. She named the baby 'Anthony', after the patron saint of lost things. Just days after the birth, the baby was taken from her arms and adopted. To all outward appearances, everything had returned to normal. Yet inside she was grieving deeply, mourning the loss of the child her body had carried, whose life she would never share and whose new name she would never know.

One thing she did know about her son, though, was his birthday. Every year, for the remaining 61 years of her life, she faced that date alone. We can only imagine the heartache and longing of a mother who was left to wonder what had become of her son. She later married and had three more children. Although her husband knew about the adoption, they made a pact never to speak of it – not even to their own children.

This story could be told many times over, with infinite variations; but in every version, love is labelled shame. When this happens, grief is silenced and stigmatized, and the grieving person is left to mourn alone.

The journey of disenfranchised grief can be slow. When shame prevents us from acknowledging the grief or seeking support from others, we are left to navigate it single-handedly. The list of losses disenfranchised by stigma is long, and many of us will be touched by shameful grief in one way or another. The source of this shame may include episodes of mental illness, imprisonment, an HIV diagnosis, addiction, reputational loss, the loss of a secret lover or suicide. We may even feel shame at grief itself: so-called 'sentimental' losses, such as the empty nest when children leave home or the death of a pet. The feeling that our grief is sentimental or indulgent can lead us to minimize the very real grief we feel.

Private grief

Disenfranchised grief is not always driven entirely by shame. Sometimes the pain simply feels too private or personal to be shared. Couples seeking treatment for infertility, for example, may not want to share their fragile hopes with friends or family; their grief over 'failed' attempts at treatment goes unrecognized.

Sometimes, those looking on might glimpse an iceberg-tip of private grief. Many years ago, I visited a man and woman who lived together in a remote village, with three lively dogs. It was the Christmas season and the shelves around their living room were crowded with cards, many depicting the scene of the nativity. On card after card, a young man and woman were shown, bent over a bed of hay, their faces lit by a golden glow from below. As I remarked (perhaps enviously) on the sheer volume of cards, the man replied, with a slight shake of his head, 'Christmas really is the revenge of the nuclear family.'

Disenfranchised grief seems particularly prevalent around infertility and baby loss. The rollercoaster journey of IVF treatment can be intensely private. It is also fraught with emotional risk: it requires a woman to invest her body and her imagination in the hope of being a mother. If this hope is dashed, she must grieve both the loss of her hoped-for baby and her projected identity. This grief is often not easy to voice.

Author Tamsin Calidas describes the day she learned that her final fertility treatment had failed. In her account, she returns to her croft on a Scottish island, after a bruising encounter at the hospital, to find a sickly newborn lamb:

> I love it, I nurture it. I spend every waking hour keeping it alive. Then one morning it is not breathing right. It dies in my arms. And that is when something breaks inside me. I cannot stop crying. I try to stop but the tears keep on flowing. It is exhausting but strangely comforting to hold the warm, dead body.[4]

It is only in recent decades that losing a baby has been widely recognized as a major bereavement. Parents suffering pregnancy loss, stillbirth, neonatal death and cot death have often been left to grieve their loss alone, with little social support or recognition of the magnitude of what has occurred. Even now, the grief of fathers can be overlooked, despite research finding that intense grief reactions tend to persist in fathers; in mothers, they more often diminish over time.[5]

Sandra was in her early 20s when she gave birth to her stillborn daughter in a district hospital in Norfolk. It was the early 1970s, and her dead baby girl was taken from her at birth: she never held her or even saw her. There were no mementoes. She learned that the baby had been buried without ceremony in a local graveyard. She named the baby Louise. Few people asked her what had become of her pregnancy; she was left to get on with life as best she could. Every year, on Louise's birthday, Sandra and her husband would quietly light a candle for their daughter.

As Louise's fortieth birthday drew near, Sandra felt that it was no longer enough to remember her in this way. She contacted the hospital chaplain and asked if, after so many years, there might be any way of finding where her daughter was buried. The hospital investigated; it found the grave site, tucked away in the corner of a municipal cemetery. It was a grave shared with two adults, unmarked by any stone, and overgrown with brambles. The chaplain arranged for the site to be cleared.

On a bright November day, Sandra and her husband met the chaplain by the graveside and participated in a bespoke ceremony that acknowledged the pain of their loss and the silence they had lived with for so long. They committed their daughter's body to the ground and prayed for her to be in God's safe keeping. Sandra was able to express her grief as never before, in a flow of healing tears. Later, they commissioned a headstone for the grave, which included Louise's name together with the names of the two adults also buried there. For years, Sandra's grief had been a restless voice, clamouring for attention; now, finally, she had been able to lay it to rest, along with her daughter.

Grief is a lonely journey: shame or secrecy only amplifies this. Others can never know the totality of our experience. The person who sits on the sofa all day or hasn't washed or eaten for a week, or who can't get off the floor – this person is experiencing acute grief, moment-by-moment, that will never be fully shared. However, there can be some relief when a supportive person builds a bridge of empathy and lets the grieving person know some part of their pain is felt and understood. Empathy is the ability to feel in microcosm what another person feels in their total experience and to communicate this understanding. Irvin Yalom calls it 'the glue of human connectedness'.[6] In the mysterious chemistry of pastoral care, we feel better when someone comes alongside us who 'gets it'.

Withholding empathy

Another factor, therefore, that may amplify the loneliness of our grief is when empathy is withheld. This can come about when we experience a loss that those around us think we should be glad about. The death of an abusive or unfaithful partner can bring up ambivalent feelings for the bereaved; it can be hard to hear comments such as 'you must be relieved' or 'good riddance'. Likewise, a divorce or break-up may be freighted with painful loss, not only of the person but also of the hopes and dreams you once shared together. Friends may not understand your grief and may expect you to feel liberated. Another loss we are told we should be glad about is the transition of a child from foster care to permanent adoptive parents; yet both the child and the foster parents are losing a special relationship. The termination of an unwanted pregnancy may be a further example of disenfranchised grief. Others may expect their friend to be glad she is out of trouble but, mixed with her relief, there may be other feelings. Although termination is not always associated with grief, for some the grief can be profound and unacknowledged.

Another version of the expectation that someone should be glad about a loss arises when others imply, 'You should be better (by now).' Friends and colleagues can signal that we need simply to 'move on' and 'try to forget it', or that we can't 'grieve for ever'. Often, we internalize these norms and feel foolish for still mourning the loss of a loved one years after the event.

Our legal systems can reinforce these messages. Employment law implicitly defines the magnitude of various losses by allowing different lengths of compassionate leave for different relationships. Typically, the death of a close family member will qualify for the longest period of compassionate leave, although it is notable that some countries exclude the death of a grandparent from this list. In 2020, the UK introduced 'Jack's Law', a commitment to provide two weeks' statutory paid bereavement leave to working parents in the event of losing a child under 18 years old or suffering a stillbirth from 24 weeks of pregnancy. This was announced by the UK Government as 'the most generous offer on parental bereavement pay and leave in the world'.[7] Here we get both messages at once: 'You should be over it; you should be glad.'

While such initiatives go some way towards acknowledging the disabling effects of acute grief, they leave much unsaid. They may give the implicit messages that the shock of grief will pass within a couple of weeks, and that we should be fit to work thereafter. They reinforce a belief that grief, and therefore empathy, have a limited shelf-life; that we 'should be better' by now and it's time for us all to move on.

Ambiguous loss

Some grief is disenfranchised because the loss itself is ambiguous. When a family member has gone missing, for example, relatives may resist grieving because it seems like a betrayal of hope. They may feel unable to grieve a situation that lacks certainty. Supporters might emphasize 'staying strong' and keeping hope alive, at the expense of acknowledging the real sense of loss they feel. Something similar can happen when a loved one changes because of mental illness, brain injury or dementia. Family and friends can feel as if they are losing the person they knew; it is a 'living bereavement'. Yet, since no one has died, the wider community may not see the depth of their grief. Likewise, when a loved one is approaching the end of life, those who are close may experience intense 'anticipatory' grief, which can be just as disabling and overwhelming as post-bereavement grief; but it may not attract the same social support.

There can be many reasons, then, why grief becomes disenfranchised. As we have seen, it can feel too shameful to acknowledge or too private to share. We might discount our grief when others think that we should be glad about the loss or when the nature of the loss remains ambiguous. Often, wider society will not issue us with 'permission' to grieve until someone has died, which overlooks the fact that loss pervades all of life. As Ken Doka reflects: 'Grief is not always about death, but it always is about attachment and separation. Any loss can engender it.'[8]

What are we to make of our disenfranchised losses? In the midst of the shame, isolation, misunderstanding and confusion of inadmissible grief, can there be any kind of spiritual goals? In the loneliness of this grief, is there room for greater connection – to self, others and the transcendent? In the shame we have identified, what deserves to be brought into the light and seen with greater clarity? And can doing battle with the voices saying what we should and shouldn't feel enable us to grow through grief? We turn here, once again, to the possibility that 'all is not loss' – to the invitation of disenfranchised grief to spiritual connection, insight and growth.

The spirituality of disenfranchised grief

Naming grief

Disenfranchised grief plays tricks. It tells us that grief is not really grief; it is something else. It is guilt, or weakness, or self-indulgence, or punishment. A spirituality that shines a light on our inner worlds and puts us more in touch with our true selves begins by *naming our response to loss* for what it is: grief.

If this were easy, we would have done it long ago. But naming grief is hard because it requires us to revisit our painful losses; we also have to dismantle the strategies we built to defend ourselves against them. When grief is disavowed and buried beneath many protective layers, we may need the patience and commitment of an archaeologist to uncover it.

Nick Duffell has worked with the 'survivors' of the British boarding school system for decades. His work is a good example of how disenfranchised grief can be named – eventually – by peeling off the defensive layers that a young person took on to survive the experience.

Duffell highlights the way that children sent to boarding schools have often been torn from the familiarity of their parents, siblings, home, school and friends. As young as seven or eight they may have been sent off to remote, often rural, 'prep' schools. Later, at around the age of 13, they may have moved on to board at one of the public schools. Typically, children in boarding schools would have shared dormitories, had little privacy, and needed to learn a new language and code of behaviour. As well as the official school rules, there were the unofficial codes and hierarchies that decided who had a right to demand services from whom. Duffell describes boys and girls who were exposed to bullying by their peers, and the risk of physical and sexual abuse by adults and older children. Secure attachment bonds between children and parents were severed; children in their first weeks at school were typically discouraged from phoning home. Stiff-upper-lipped parents (who may themselves have been brutalized by the same treatment) often justified sending away their young children to boarding school with the claim that the experience would be 'the making of them'.

In his book of that title, Nick Duffell identifies three 'strategic survival personalities' adopted by young people to survive.[9] He labels these the 'conformist', the 'rebel' and the 'crushed'. Each is a defensive strategy for children trying to cope with the denial of their deep feelings of grief at being torn from the security of a familiar family and environment, and separated from the bonds of love that sustained them. Children are often led to expect that they will have a wonderful time ('It will be just like Hogwarts') and, by implication, that feelings to the contrary can't be trusted. Consequently, a child's sadness, anxiety and grief are pushed out of sight. As the saying goes, 'Big boys don't cry.' Duffell quotes one boy's letter home to his mother, where he writes, 'I hope you're not missing me, because I'm certainly not missing you.' We can sense, beneath these words of apparent reassurance, a world of unacknowledged anger, grief and pain.

How can boarding school survivors learn to name their grief? How can any of us? We have to be prepared to peel back our protective layers and acknowledge our vulnerable selves. We need to lift off old bandages and tend the wound of loss. It may be hard to name grief as *grief* – to spot it hiding beneath our decades-long amnesia – yet our tell-tale fixed smiles, emotional numbness or breezy activism may point to a wound untended. It may be that the help of another is required before we are able to name it. A counsellor or therapist can be a trusted companion, a fellow archaeologist who will gently help us to brush back the layers. There is a view among therapists that all therapy leads back to loss in one form or another. In this sense, helping people to name disenfranchised grief is at the core of what therapists do.

Voicing our guilt and shame

We have seen that guilt often follows grief around, like a nagging partner. Where grief is disenfranchised, shame, too, lurks in the shadows, waiting to expose us. Guilt and shame are not symptoms of a healthy spirituality. If spirituality is partly about forming a truer connection to ourselves and the world as we find it, guilt and shame do the opposite. Guilt assails us with a barrage of ways we *should* have acted, while shame silences us with its threats of exposure and embarrassment.

Guilt and shame feed on silence. When silence rules, grief dare not speak its name. But if we can learn to *voice our guilt and shame*, its power can quickly diminish. I have noticed the visible relief of bereaved people when they hear one another speak of their guilt in a group setting. Our own feelings of guilt around the death of a loved one may *seem* deserved; but when we hear someone else describe their feelings of guilt, these often strike us as irrational. How could she have known her father would die in that hour while she snatched some sleep? How could he have known that the unkind word he said to his partner that morning would be the last thing he ever said to her? Voicing feelings of guilt can help to repel the attack of self-blame we launch on ourselves.

Noticing that guilt is a common (and often irrational) response to grief can also normalize the experience for us and help us to gain some perspective on it. The invitation of grief, as we cower in guilty silence, is an invitation to bring our guilt and shame into the light and speak openly about it with others who are safe enough. This may be the beginning of a journey in which we learn to be more open about other shameful parts of ourselves, too; one in which we learn to be more reconciled to ourselves and discover that we can be valued by others not only in our strength, but also in our vulnerability.

Of course, not all guilt and shame are irrational. When we break our own moral codes, we may feel our guilt is warranted. Guilt and shame are not all bad: they tell us that different parts of us are in conflict; they help to regulate our behaviour and socialize us within wider society. Sometimes a confession can be liberating. Therapists, trusted friends, bereavement groups, faith leaders and spiritual directors, among others, may be able to offer an absolving witness to our guilt and shame.

Accepting ourselves

Often grief remains disenfranchised because we believe that our grief is unacceptable. It exposes us in some way. We fear that if others knew of our lost loves, our childlike tears, our ancient wounds or any of the other vulnerable nooks of the self where grief lurks, we would be humiliated. Often, we can hardly bear to look at these things ourselves.

Our shame can be reinforced by the stories we tell ourselves. Believing our grief is unacceptable, we tell ourselves we are weak or stupid for feeling this way. We blame ourselves, drawing a fixed arrow from the fact that *something* went wrong to a belief that *we* are what's wrong. We tell ourselves that we don't deserve to grieve or that we should be over it by now. These stories leave us feeling exposed and fearing that, at any moment, we may be found out.

We may have little insight into this split in our personalities: as Richard Rohr observes, 'Your False Self is who you think you are.'[10] The true self, by contrast, may be so well protected that we can only discern faint signs of its existence. Carl Jung saw one such clue in our observation of children:

> the sight of a child ... will arouse certain longings in adult, civilised persons – longings that relate to the unfulfilled desires and needs of those parts of the personality that have been blotted out of the total picture in favour of the adopted persona.[11]

Children therefore pose a threat to the 'survival personality' by reminding us of the wounded self, the younger part of us that we have so carefully buried; or they bring to mind the happy and playful person we were before the trauma broke. Children may whisper rumours of Eden. It is perhaps no wonder, then, that the British boarding school treats children as 'incompetent', 'un-made' and 'in the way' – mere 'premature adults';[12] no wonder the British have said that they should be 'seen and not heard'. The reminder they bring of the loss of the true, spontaneous self may be too threatening. Throwing off false guilt and shame might involve reacquainting ourselves with a younger part of us: learning to love and parent the wounded child within and re-integrating the heedless sense of fun, creativity and confidence.

The false self protects us but ultimately it doesn't serve us well. While it may protect us from shame-filled grief, it prevents us from truly grieving. The false self cuts us off from the created bedrock of our personalities and causes us to live as if we were the characters we have written for ourselves. This false self may manifest in such guises as the breezy but brittle executive, the extrovert but secretive gay man, or the dynamic but wistful mother.

Healthy spirituality begins from the world as we find it, and that includes the self. The grief we carry from multiple wounds contains an invitation to look squarely at our losses – especially the secret and shameful ones – and to own our feelings of grief. Instead of fleeing the scene, can we stay with our painful memories – a break-up, a failure, a poor decision, a regret, a wound – and accept that this is part of our story?

Rituals of grieving

Disenfranchised grief is invisible. If we are to overcome the silence and isolation it so often imposes on us, we need to find ways to 'speak its name'. One powerful way to do this is to perform a ritual that will acknowledge the grief. Ritual acts are as old as humanity; in our religious traditions, we can find bereavement rituals, which have been forged and honed over millennia, that can touch the roots of our psyche.

In recent decades, western societies have moved away from traditional institutional expressions of grieving towards constructing more individual, do-it-yourself rituals. While doing so may ensure a more personal approach, the disadvantage is that mourners are often trying to construct a bespoke service under pressure of time and in the midst of shock and grief. If grieving rituals sometimes miss the mark, it may be partly because time-honoured words and rituals have been supplanted by whatever words come near the top of an Internet search. Perhaps it is no wonder that there is an increasing trend towards direct cremation, which bypasses the messy business of coffins and funeral services and cuts straight to the 'celebration' event. No doubt this is partly to do with funeral poverty; but I wonder if it is also psychologically convenient: finding meaningful rituals that work, and facing the emotional task of performing them, may feel too hard for some.

Yet grieving rituals are important and short-circuiting them can be harmful. When working with bereaved people, I often ask if there has been a funeral. I am listening for clues that the person has been present and able to say goodbye when the body of a loved one disappears behind a curtain or pall, or into a grave. Sometimes, those who have been unable to witness this ritual moment can feel stuck in their grieving and unable to accept that the person has died. The barring of children from funerals, more common in the past, may have been particularly harmful here.

Rituals help us to attend to disenfranchised grief and to work through it. Grief that has been disallowed in some way can be validated and normalized in the ritual act. As we saw in Sandra's story, the graveside ritual for a stillborn baby, 40 years after her birth, brought healing and closure to Sandra's grief. As a hospital chaplain, I was sometimes called to the labour ward to hold and bless the body of a baby who had been stillborn. Usually, with the parents and close family gathered around, I held the tiny remains of a lost lifetime of hopes and loves, and fumbled for words that could touch the truth of their pain. I often used some set prayers (with the parents' consent) but found that every occasion demanded some adjustment. I said a blessing for child and parents. Sometimes I gave the parents a beautiful pebble to take and hold in their distress; it served as a reminder of the moment and a solid witness to the fact that their son or daughter had come into the world. Sometimes I gave them a little candle to keep in their memory box and light on the anniversary of their child's birth. This was a way of acknowledging that the child would never be forgotten and that their sadness would have no expiry date.

Simple rituals such as this can help us to acknowledge grief and name it as such. They provide a bridge between the mess of our loss and a larger meaning, which sets our loss in context. As Francis Weller notes, communal rituals both contain our grief and enable us to release it.[13] The word 'religion' may derive from the Latin *religare*, 'to bind': symbolic rituals have the power to gather up and bind together the fragments of our shattered experience into something meaningful we can express. It may be the letter we write to an abusive parent, which we burn and scatter with their ashes. We may choose to participate in a larger ritual, such as the AIDS Memorial Quilt, a 50,000-panel memorial that has helped to destigmatize deaths from AIDS since the 1980s.[14] It may be as simple as a stone thrown into the sea, to acknowledge a lost relationship that we now choose to relinquish. Whatever rituals we adopt, they can provide a visible and symbolic expression of our disenfranchised grief; they can help it to become the grief that dares to speak its name.

Notes

1 K. J. Doka, 2017, *Grief Is a Journey: Finding your path through loss*, New York, NY: Atria Books, p. 183.

2 Stonewall, 2014, *Planning for Later Life: A guide for lesbian, gay and bisexual people*, Manchester: Stonewall and the Cooperative Funeral Care.

3 Lord Alfred Douglas, 2018, 'Two Loves', *The Collected Poems of Lord Alfred Douglas*, London: Forgotten Books.

4 T. Calidas, 2020, *I Am an Island*, London: Doubleday, p. 92.

5 M. J. McNeil, J. N. Baker, I. Snyder, A. R. Rosenberg and E. C. Kaye, 'Grief and Bereavement in Fathers after the Death of a Child: A systematic review', *Pediatrics*, 147/4 (2021), p. e2020040386, at https://doi.org/10.1542/peds.2020-040386.

6 I. D. Yalom, 2008, *Staring at the Sun: Being at peace with your own mortality*, London: Piatkus, p. 123.

7 UK Government, 2020, 'UK Set to Introduce "Jack's Law" – New Legal Right to Paid Parental Bereavement Leave', GOV.UK, at https://www.gov.uk/government/news/uk-set-to-introduce-jacks-law-new-legal-right-to-paid-parental-bereavement-leave, accessed 14.04.2025.

8 Doka, *Grief Is a Journey*, p. 197.

9 N. Duffell, 2000, *The Making of Them: The British attitude to children and the boarding school system*, London: Lone Arrow Press.

10 R. Rohr, 2013, *Immortal Diamond: The search for our true self*, London: SPCK, p. 36.

11 C. Jung, 1995, *Memories, Dreams, Reflections*, London: Fontana, pp. 272–3.

12 Duffell, *Making of Them*, p. 8.

13 F. Weller, 2015, *The Wild Edge of Sorrow: Rituals of renewal and the sacred work of grief*, Berkeley, CA: North Atlantic Books, pp. 73f.

14 National AIDS Memorial, 2024, 'Interactive AIDS Quilt', at https://www.aidsmemorial.org/interactive-aids-quilt, accessed 14.04.2025.

8

Regret

> You cannot step twice into the same river.
> (Heraclitus, *c*. fifth century BCE)

Life demands we make choices. Early in our adult lives we may experience choice as freedom, the intoxicating sense that the future offers an unlimited palette of options. Our choice of courses, partners, jobs, locations and lifestyles seems to lie open before us. The future is unmade; our ambitions untested. We can easily believe the popular wisdom that says you can be anything you want to be.

As the years roll by, our choices come to be fringed with anxiety. We begin to sense that, while we could do anything, we can't do everything. Every fork in the road takes us one way and not another. As William James wrote more than a century ago, 'every end of desire that presents itself appears exclusive of some other end of desire. Shall a man ... follow his fancy for Amelia, *or* for Henrietta? – both cannot be the choice of his heart.'[1] As our choices are made, we begin to set a course, to fix our bearings. For some, the fear of excluding one option prevents a choice being made altogether. We are impaled on the horns of an existential dilemma: choose one thing and miss out on another; choose nothing and miss out on both.

As time passes, we may become more aware that time is one-directional and finite. We cannot turn the clock back to a fork in the road and retake a decision; nor do we have endless years in which to try out multiple alternatives. Regrets accumulate; options diminish. Looking back, Joe Moran observed: 'Very gradually, and without you noticing at first, your life began to shrink.'[2]

When I first began working in the NHS, I found myself asking why I had never pursued a career as a doctor, like my grandfather. I had been fairly good at science at school; with a lot of hard work, I thought I might have qualified. It was a trainee doctor in his early 40s who delivered the shock. He informed me that the upper age limit for training was 45; at the time, I was 47. A door had closed; I'd missed the boat. Although I had no real intention of changing career, it was the vanishing of an option that rocked me.

Regret for the greener grass

Choosing means losing. Every choice excludes. If, for much of the time, we are happy with our choices, we might not even notice the loss. But inevitably, as our decisions multiply, we begin to accumulate regrets. Sometimes we regret our actions; but, more often, we regret our omissions. It is the unchosen path that haunts us most.

When we exclude one option by choosing another, we can't help but wonder what would have happened. We return in memory to the fork in the road; we gaze longingly down the unchosen path, ruminating on the 'what ifs': what if I'd chosen Amelia? What if I'd taken the geology degree? What if I'd been truer to myself? Wondering what *would* have happened is a complex form of loss because it involves missing a road we never took: an option that only ever existed as a possibility. It is regret for the greener grass.

In recent years, the volume has been turned up on the potential for missing out. Idealized versions of people living their 'best lives' are posted on social media; they cause us to spiral into frantic hypervigilance, as we cast around to see what others are doing and wonder how much of life is passing us by. Writing in the magazine of the Harvard Business School in 2004, Patrick McGinnis coined the acronym FOMO to describe this modern anxiety: fear of missing out. The term has since become commonplace. The social media panopticon has ensured we are exposed to relentless choice anxiety.

Ideals and duties

Our grass-is-greener regrets can be examined further. Research suggests we are more likely to resolve those regrets when we have failed in our duties, rather than when we have failed to live up to our ideals.[3] The regrets we are left with, in other words, more often concern the ways in which we have failed *ourselves*: the dreams we didn't pursue; the authentic self we cramped to fit the expectations of others; the courage we failed to grasp.

Bronnie Ware is an Australian author who worked in palliative care for many years. She observed the kinds of regret that people express at the end of life. In 2019, she published a best-seller, which had the title *The Top Five Regrets of the Dying*.[4] All five began with the words, 'I wish …'. Patients expressed regrets about not being true to themselves; they had worked too hard; they had not had the courage to express their feelings; they had lost touch with friends; they could have let themselves be happier. All five are regrets about a failure to live up to ideals – even the one about 'working too hard', which is pregnant with regret for misspent time and lost opportunity. All five are filled with longing and wonder: 'What if I'd let more of me be me?'

Regret is a form of loss and, like all loss, it asks to be grieved. This leaves me wondering two things. First, how do we go about grieving our regrets? I think of shame-filled actions that are buried in an irrecoverable past; or longings to go back and do things differently, when the people who matter are long gone. And second, where does our grief take us? Can the grief for our bitterest regrets be in any way transformative? Can we find embers in the ashes – evidence, perhaps, that 'all is not loss'?

Regret and spiritual transformation

Naming our losses

How do we mourn our regrets? As we saw in the previous chapter, the first step in grieving is to name what we have lost. This can be difficult, because regret comes in many guises and may not point us towards any obvious loss.

The losses we experience from our harmful omissions can be particularly hard to name. I notice that bereaved people are often burdened with a sense of guilt about things they 'failed' to do in the time leading up to their loved one's death. They may believe they failed to spot the early signs of cancer; they didn't advocate for better care in hospital; they failed to bring their loved one home to die; they were absent at the moment of death. These can be sources of bitter regret. The obvious loss of the person is compounded by the loss of a better ending, a longer life, a more peaceful death, and the dying person's wishes being respected. And, once again, we may have to deal with the wound to our self-concept that our omissions have made, as we come to terms with feeling a failure as a son, daughter, partner or friend.

Naming these losses allows us to grieve them. Feelings of guilt are often not easy to shift, however, and it can take time to put them in perspective. When we cling to irrational guilt, it may be because we prefer to believe that we could have changed the outcome rather than to accept we were helpless in the face of a loved one's suffering and death. When this is so, we can only back out of our guilt and regret by returning to face our helplessness. This recognition may be frightening at first but, ultimately, it names an important part of our loss.

Other guilt may feel more justified; we may have failed to live up to our own values. Some religious traditions provide effective rituals to help us deal with guilt. Whether or not these are available to us, we still must learn to 'live with ourselves'. As we shall see later, one way we might begin to address our past is by cultivating *compassionate hindsight*. As Francis Weller suggests, 'Regrets require the soft hands of self-compassion.'[5]

REGRET

Keeping vigil at the fork in the road

Coming to terms with the ways we have wounded others can be a difficult task. Yet, as we have seen, our deepest regrets seem to arise from those circumstances where we have neglected our own needs and silenced our dreams.

Perhaps we look back to a watershed moment in life, where we chose one thing and not another. I think of the woman who gave up the hope of a university degree to stay home and look after a demanding and manipulative mother. I think of the man who entered his father's business, helping to run a factory in the North of England, when the cry of his heart had been to become an actor and writer. Or perhaps there was never a watershed choice, but a series of little decisions that congealed into decades of becoming habitually stuck. Many women I have worked with, for example, have felt themselves unable to break free from the orbit of a partner who was silent, abusive, narcissistic or controlling.

As we return to the fork in the road and look with longing at the unchosen path, it can be hard to quantify what we have lost. For some, our regret may be for a missed opportunity. But what might have followed from this we can only guess: greater happiness, fulfilment, autonomy or satisfaction? Who knows? That is part of the agony of regret: we don't quite know what we have missed. It is all too easy to fill this vacuum with sunny visions of a better life without noticing that we have set up an unfair contest between fantasy and reality.

The Australian cartoonist Michael Leunig captures this dilemma brilliantly in a simple cartoon. It depicts a glum looking man, hands in pockets, walking along the pavement of a dark street fringed with tall, windowless buildings. He is passing the mouth of an alley. Light is pouring from the alley and spilling across his path. His head is turning to peer down the alley as he passes it. On the corners of the buildings, above his head, are two street signs. The dark street he is walking along is named 'THE LIFE YOU LEAD'. The name of the sun-filled alley is 'THE LIFE YOU COULD HAVE LED'.

The life you could have led is the life that haunts you. Searching behaviour is a common expression of grief; many of us keep vigil at the fork in the road and wonder what might have happened if we had taken a different route. Perhaps we are aware of those times when we struck it lucky: a chance meeting led to an important contact or a critical piece of information; and from the slightest thread, we hauled in the net that held our future. But at the fork in the road, the same thought can torment us: which threads did we miss?

I was fortunate to be at university in the boom years of the 1980s, before the recession of 1991. At that time, the 'milk round' was still in operation. Representatives from the world of finance, industry and the public sector set up stall in Oxford to lure 'talent' to their workforces. My fellow students told stories of being schmoozed in smart London hotels by executives from major corporations. Others found fast-track careers in the BBC or were buttonholed for opportunities in the diplomatic service. 'Try everything' seemed to be the mantra. At the very least, you would get a free lunch.

For reasons that still escape me, I didn't go. Perhaps I had a fixed idea of what I wanted. Perhaps I recoiled from being lured into anything. But for many years, this became a regret; a tantalizing fork in the road where the world spilled golden opportunities at my feet and I unthinkingly walked away.

Missing persons

Sometimes the fork in the road is not about a missed opportunity, but a missing person. A relationship breaks up or hardly begins; a friendship grows cold. We move on and perhaps lose touch. Years pass; among the crowd of faces we have mostly forgotten, one or two still stand out. We wonder what happened to them and can't quite let them go. We may feel more than curiosity; we may have a sense of longing or pining, perhaps. For some, this feeling may flame into an obsession: a compulsive desire to recover the person. However intensely felt, the sense of there being a missing person can lead us back to the fork in the road to keep vigil and wonder.

Sitting next to me as I write is a large cardboard box full of letters. I sealed up the box about thirty years ago. Over the past three decades, it has moved with me from place to place, living in cupboards under the stairs or doing service as a makeshift coffee table. Recently, I opened it and began to read. Letters spilled out: letters from my dead mother; letters from old friends; letters from teenage girlfriends, which told the whole story from infatuation to break-up. I didn't get far in my curiosity: the past is a demanding read. The open box came to feel like a dark well down which I was falling, hitting the emotional water-table 30 years below.

Inevitably, there were regrets. Old wounds and passions I had long forgotten came alive. I felt the urge to return to forks in the road, to look people up, to wonder what *would* have happened. I longed to apply the emotional tools I have now to try to understand what took place in relationships back then. I found myself in the guilty pursuit of lost loves and friendships, searching for clues online that would make sense of my unchosen paths, my unlived life.

Re-membering

One day, as I returned to one of these forks in the road to tend my wistful regrets, I came to an abrupt realization: *I am not searching for them; I am searching for me.*

So often, at a fork in the road, we leave a little of ourselves behind. We choose between parts of ourselves. Perhaps we choose a helping profession over a career in a creative industry because the caring and nurturing part of us is prominent. But in leaving the creative option behind, at the fork in the road, what have we denied in ourselves? The artist? The risk-taker? The entrepreneur? Keeping vigil at the fork in the road can be an opportunity to discover parts of us we left behind there. We can't recover the unchosen path or person: they, too, will have changed. But we can recover those parts of ourselves that we disowned back then in the compromise of choosing. Remembering can become an opportunity to *re-member* ourselves; to recover the limbs of the soul.

The fork in the road is bittersweet. By returning to it, we may be filled with longing for the unchosen path, the unloved partner, the unexplored career: in sum, what Jung called the 'unlived life'.[6] The path we never took is like a little death: we can no more follow it than we can follow our loved ones beyond the grave. To move on, we need to grieve the unlived life: the years we will never get back. Yet, when we recognize that our search is often for left-behind parts of ourselves, it matters less that we cannot return in time to the fork in the road. Instead, our regrets can become a rich source of information about the parts of ourselves that need to be tended. If we can take an unflinching look at our regrets – including the pain and the shame – we can better hear their call to a more authentic and abundant way of living. Regrets can become our allies. They cease to be the bad guys if we can treat them as sherpas on the climb to maturity.

Alone and unrehearsed: existential regret

Another loss that comes with regret is the realization that the life we lead is our one and only life. We might call this realization *existential regret*. At first sight, this looks a lot like the wound of mortality we considered in Chapter 2. This loss comes about as we realize that our lives are finite; we don't have endless years in which to pursue our dreams.

Yet there is something more here. The sting of regret also consists in the fact that there is no going back and no undoing of the past. As the self-help slogan proclaims, *life is not a rehearsal*. In fact, it is more like an extended jazz improvisation in which we must learn to play our instrument during a live performance. There are no parallel lives we can lead in which we can first make our mistakes, before stepping out in front of an audience. All the world's a stage; and we must live our seven ages without rehearsal. Nor can we pause the action on the reality-show of our lives or rewind a few scenes to try them again. Regret reminds us that we travel through life on a one-way, non-refundable ticket; and we have only one life. At best, we can attempt to repair our mistakes or try something different in the future. Heraclitus' maxim holds true: 'You cannot step twice into the same river.'[7]

Further, regret, like other forms of suffering, reminds us that we live and die alone. It is not that we may not have friends or family who can empathize with our regrets and support us; it is simply that we cannot outsource the management of our pain. Will Self, reflecting from hospital on his serious illness, wrote, 'When you realise you may very well die … you realise something else you have always known but heavily repressed: your death is all your own.'[8] Regret, like dying, is a form of solitary confinement. Somehow, I must learn to live with my decisions, my actions, my omissions. Humanly speaking, no one else can bear them for me.

These are uncomfortable realizations, hard existential facts that poke out like bedrock. Like the wound of mortality, the singularity of our lives can be hard to accept – both the one-way ticket and the loneliness of the ride. We find ways to cloak this truth. We attempt to live parallel lives, perhaps through our children, or by having affairs or second homes. Maybe we try to outrun the marching years with a fresh start: moving abroad, cosmetic surgery or pursuing a vision of the good life. Perhaps we keep our companions close, so we feel less alone and less at risk. These only work for so long. Eventually, each of us must lose these illusions and confront the existential rock face: you have one life; your pain is your own.

True spiritual wisdom deals in the hard facts of existence and does not try to dodge them. Like the wound of mortality, we need to grieve the wound of our regrets, particularly those that are now irreversible. Yet, even as we grieve this dimension of existential regret, we may hear an invitation to personal growth and transforming insight. How might we hear this?

Compassionate hindsight

Spirituality, as we have seen, is about accepting what is; it is not about trying to pretend the world is the way we would like it to be. The pain of regret may invite us to discover greater self-compassion as we reflect on the flawed and limited human being that meets us in the mirror. Each of us is dealt a hand in life, and our cards are not all equal. Both nature and nurture can leave us impoverished in certain ways. I wonder if, at root, our regrets are not so much about the *way* we behave as about the fact that we are the kind of people who tend to behave that way. This boils down to something personal and painful: 'I regret being me.'

Compassionate hindsight is the active cultivation of an attitude towards the self that says, 'You did your best with the limited resources and insights you had at the time. Like every human being, you made mistakes. *You played your cards from the hand you were dealt.* You did not choose your hand.' Self-compassion counsels us: 'Accept your limitations. Forgive your mistakes. Relinquish the hope of a better past, but remember you are not bound to repeat it. You are not the sum total of the critical things you have told yourself: you are unique, beautifully human and of infinite worth.' This kind of self-compassion can be transformative when we develop it into a habit, displacing our self-critical narratives. It might be worth speaking these words to the mirror, slowly, while keeping in mind a significant regret and noticing what arises within you.

Necessary regret

Another way we might reframe our existential regrets is to see them as evidence that we have been privileged with good options. Often the choices we make are between two or more paths that look equally promising. A young person joins the police, but they could have joined the fire service. A couple could have adopted a child, but they decide instead to invest their energy in a social enterprise. Choices such as these are unavoidable. Even if it is true that we could become anything, the fact remains that we can't become everything. The person who joins the police might regret missing out on opportunities they could have had in the fire service and vice versa. But these are necessary regrets: they are evidence that we had good-enough options. As I get older, I find myself increasingly reflecting on choices I didn't make and wondering what would have happened. Sometimes, in an idle conversation, my wife and I plot the moves we could have made and weigh up the pros and cons of long-extinct options. Often, these reveries end with a knowing smile and one of us pronouncing, 'Lives we didn't lead.' These regrets have lost their sting, for the most part, because we recognize that we had no choice but to choose. We chose one option over another, and both options seemed good enough.

Regret as a badge of honour

In an ideal world, would we wish to reach the end of our lives able to say that we had *no regrets*? It is an interesting thought experiment. What would a life with no regrets look like? At first sight, it might seem that this verdict would be the crowning of a successful life – every decision made was the best option, no serious mistakes were made, and nothing of importance was left out. Yet, apart from being unrealistic, I wonder if such a life might not be as attractive as it first appears. A life with no regrets suggests a life in which we failed to wrestle with life's inevitable choices, took few risks, had few good options, and desired little of importance. Far from being a successful life, a life with no regrets sounds like one that was sterile and anaemic. Another way, then, that we might reframe our existential regrets is to see them as a badge of honour: evidence that we turned up in our lives and have the scars to prove it. Looked at this way, regrets are the bruises we bear from our courageous wrestling in the arena of life. As Nick Cave observes: 'They are generally indicators of a certain self-awareness or personal growth or distance travelled.'[9]

Avoiding future regret

One further way that regret might prove transformative is when we change course to avoid a repeat of our regret.

Maintaining the belief that our present life is a rehearsal for a 'real life' that will begin at some point in the future is a defence against regret, and ultimately death, that may serve us for a while. In James Patterson's novel, *Sam's Letters to Jennifer*, Sam stumbles across a scribbled quote, attributed to a priest, Fr Alfred D'Souza:

> For a long time it had seemed to me that life was about to begin – real life. But there was always some obstacle in the way, something to be got through first, some unfinished business, time still to be served, a debt to be paid. Then life would begin. At last it dawned on me that these obstacles were my life.[10]

Many of us live with a sense that our present life is somehow provisional, a stepping-stone to the real thing. 'I never savoured life for what it was,' wrote James Robertson's enigmatic minister, Gideon Mack. 'I only wanted to get the next stage of it.'[11] Joan Didion confessed to a similar malaise: 'I was in a curious position in New York: it never occurred to me that I was living a real life there. In my imagination I was always there for just another few months.'[12]

Postponing our lives in this way protects us from the disappointment of regret. If whatever we decide to do turns out to have been a mistake, it doesn't matter, we can tell ourselves, because real life has not yet begun. If we keep on postponing 'real life', we think, we will have little to lose. As Sigmund Freud's colleague Otto Rank expressed it: 'Some refuse the loan of life to avoid the debt of death.'[13]

Yet this defence only works for so long. At some point, the realization catches up with us that we have been absent from our lives while waiting for the real thing to begin. Far from avoiding regrets, the perpetual postponement of life is likely to be storing them up. Becoming aware of the ways in which we put our lives on hold can wake us up to the fact that we are literally wishing our lives away. Acknowledging regret at living an untenanted existence can give each of us new impetus to inhabit the one and only life we have.

Nietzsche advocated we undertake a thought experiment in which we imagine our lives being repeated again and again for ever. If we knew that our whole lives, or even the next year, were doomed to repetition, how might we live differently? It can be a powerful experiment: it leaves no room for postponing life and confronts us with the responsibility we have for the choices we make. Perhaps we would come to address the 'regrets of the dying' sooner? In our eternally recurring year, might we become truer to ourselves, less in thrall to work, more emotionally spontaneous, more careful to nurture friendships, and happier? This thought experiment jolts us into awareness, creating a shift in consciousness not unlike the impact of a crisis in the ordinary course of life. It invokes what the theologian Eugene Peterson has called 'voluntary disaster': the deliberate creation of conditions in which we come to our senses. 'Why wait for an accident, an illness, a failure?'[14]

Regret, as we have seen, is a peculiarly solitary form of loss. In our final chapter, we turn from this individual loss to the losses we share in our human communities. Loss can be carried from one generation to another; it may extend through space as whole communities come to terms with the erosion of precious cultural and environmental treasures. We will think about the grief that arises when we forget we are creatures of soil and soul.

Notes

1 W. James, 1897, *The Will to Believe and Other Essays in Popular Philosophy*, London: Longmans, Green, and Co. [online facsimile], Project Gutenberg (release date 8 May 2009), at https://www.gutenberg.org/files/26659/26659-h/26659-h.htm.

2 J. Moran, 2021, *If You Should Fail: Why success eludes us and why it doesn't matter*, London: Penguin, p. 132.

3 S. Davidai and T. Gilovich, 'The Ideal Road not Taken: The self-discrepancies involved in people's most enduring regrets', *Emotion*, 18/3 (2018), pp. 439–52, at https://doi.org/10.1037/emo0000326, accessed 14.04.2025.

4 B. Ware, 2019, *The Top Five Regrets of the Dying: A life transformed by the dearly departing*, London: Hay House UK.

5 F. Weller, 2015, *The Wild Edge of Sorrow: Rituals of renewal and the sacred work of grief*, Berkeley, CA: North Atlantic Books, p. 43.

6 C. G. Jung, 1975, *Structure and Dynamics of the Psyche: The collected works of C. G. Jung*, vol. 8, trans. R. F. C. Hull, Princeton: Princeton University Press, p. 518, at https://jungiancenter.org/wp-content/uploads/2023/09/vol-8-the-structure-and-dynamics-of-the-psyche.pdf, accessed 14.04.2025.

7 B. Russell, 1961, *History of Western Philosophy and Its Connection with Political and Social Circumstances from the Earliest Times to the Present Day*, London: Routledge, p. 63.

8 Will Self, 2024, 'Reclusion', *Illuminated* [podcast], BBC Radio 4, at https://www.bbc.co.uk/sounds/play/m0024cvm, accessed 14.04.2025.

9 N. Cave and S. O'Hagan, 2023, *Faith, Hope and Carnage*, Edinburgh: Canongate Books, p. 207.

10 J. Patterson, 2004, *Sam's Letters to Jennifer*, London: Headline, p. 77.

11 J. Robertson, 2007, *The Testament of Gideon Mack*, London: Penguin, p. 28.

12 J. Didion, 2017, *Slouching towards Bethlehem*, London: 4th Estate, p. 230.

13 Quoted in I. D. Yalom, 2008, *Staring at the Sun: Being at peace with your own mortality*, London: Piatkus, p. 109.

14 E. H. Peterson, 1994, *Under the Unpredictable Plant: An exploration in vocational holiness*, Grand Rapids, MI: Eerdmans, p. 90.

9

Forgetting

Our sadness is almost an aesthetic response – appropriate because we have marred a great, mad, profligate work of art, taken a hammer to the most perfectly proportioned of sculptures. (Bill McKibben, *An Idea Can Go Extinct*)[1]

Loss shadows us from birth to death. It is the story of our lives. But as well as feeling the pain of our own personal losses, we draw from a shared well of sorrow. In this chapter, we turn from individual to collective grief. As human beings, we share the grief of losses that afflict us on a global scale, that stretch back through generations. 'Our personal experiences of loss and suffering', writes the psychotherapist Francis Weller, 'are now bound inextricably with dying coral reefs, melting polar caps, the silencing of languages, the collapse of democracy, and the fading of civilization.'[2]

Collective grief comes in many forms, but I want to think about two in particular: the loss that comes from forgetting who we are as animal bodies embedded in the natural world; and the loss that arises from losing touch with our shared experience of the sacred. C. S. Lewis described these two aspects of human life as *bios* and *zoe*.[3] These are Greek terms that make a rough distinction between biological and spiritual life: between soil and soul. Although these two forms of amnesia might not at first appear related, I will argue that they have common roots and are part of the same malaise. Those of us living in western 'civilization' are caught up in a collective enchantment that has caused us to forget something of what it means to be human.

When we forget who we are, we suffer a loss of identity. Much of our contemporary discontent can be traced, I suggest, to our disconnection from soil and soul: we have forgotten our roots in the organic stuff of which we are made; we have also lost touch with communal traditions and the realm of the sacred. Europeans belong to what Danièle Hervieu-Léger describes as 'amnesiac societies', suspended between heaven and earth but rooted in neither. 'We yearn for connection with one another and with the soul,' writes Alastair McIntosh. 'But we forget that, like the earthworm, we too are an organism of the soil. We too need grounding.'[4]

Modernity and amnesia

The story of our amnesia goes back centuries. Our break with the sacred world can be traced back to processes of secularization in western Europe that emerged from the seventeenth century onwards. Our break with the natural world is more recent and is commonly located at the beginning of the Industrial Revolution, now treated as the baseline event for the measurement of global warming.

The 'twin cumbersome nouns'[5] of industrialization and urbanization point to the most significant processes of modernity that have helped us to forget our roots in soil and soul. As the French sociologist Gabriel Le Bras noted, 'out of a hundred villagers who settle in Paris, roughly ninety will cease to be churchgoers by the time they step out of the Gare Montparnasse'.[6] I have told the story of modernity's role in secularization elsewhere.[7] What matters here is simply to notice that the modern world has disrupted our millennia-old connection to the earth, to one another and to the sacred. Modernity enabled social relations to be disembedded from local settings and reconfigured across time and space. Relationships in community came to be replaced with relationships mediated by technology, bureaucracy and surveillance, in what Anthony Giddens has characterized as the 'transformation of intimacy'.[8]

FORGETTING

In addition to these social processes, we have inherited the ideological legacy of the Enlightenment, a core belief of which is that humanity is continually making progress – not only in knowledge but in civilization.[9] We have imbibed this myth, together with its linear view of history. It has become so embedded in our language that the metaphor 'going forwards' is used unthinkingly to mean 'in the future'. For some traditional societies, however, you *back* into the future, since you cannot see it; it is only as it unfolds that it becomes visible in front of you.[10] Based on this view, the past is a rich source of wisdom for present living, which is a contrast to our western tendency to laugh at the 'primitive' ways of our forebears. We believe that we are caught up in progress; it is harder to imagine that we may be accelerating towards our demise. Our future-oriented mindset makes it easier to neglect the past and, ultimately, to forget it.

Although this story goes back centuries, in another sense our break with the natural and sacred worlds is alarmingly recent. Steffi Bednarek observes: 'We only have to go back eight to ten generations to find relatives in the lineages of contemporary white Europeans who experienced the breakage in the connection to Nature, to the cycles of the seasons and to traditions that provided communal containers for collective experiences.'[11]

As a species, we have not had time to adjust. If the backdrop of 300,000 years of human history were compressed into a single human lifespan of 70 years, the Industrial Revolution would have begun just three weeks ago. In that time, we have altered the climate and ecology on which we depend for our survival. We are like school children conducting gas experiments from inside a closed fume cupboard. Our experiment with secularization is similarly novel. Across the globe, through most of history, people have accepted the sacred as a fact of life: secular Europe is an exception. We have forgotten that our lives are *bios* and *zoe*; we belong to soil and soul. It is as if we are living in exile, with only the dimmest memory of home.

To some, the advent of the modern world might seem taken for granted and unproblematic. Certainly, we can't turn back the clock; nor do I want to romanticize the past. I have no desire to live in a society that lacks anaesthetics and religious tolerance. Yet, beneath our comfortable lives, the grief we feel at our disconnection from nature and the numinous is real, hidden in plain sight. In some cases, it is more than disconnection; it amounts to trauma that has been normalized in our bargain with modernity. We have gained the whole world but lost our *soul* – by which I mean lost touch with our interiority, with our deepest values, and with the wisdom traditions once embodied in our communities. The fact that we struggle even to see this loss is, itself, a symptom of our condition. Only by remembering and grieving our collective losses can we learn to live on the planet with redemptive humility.

In this chapter, I want to take a closer look at these forms of collective grief – nature grief and soul grief – that have come about through forgetting our roots. They are forms of exile, the pain of which is felt in such symptoms as loneliness, isolation, lack of meaning and fulfilment, a loss of connection to place and ancestry, climate anxiety, environmental grief, and a restless longing for the sacred. These are ultimately collective griefs; it may be that their healing can only come about through shared rituals and understandings. If we ignore them, they will remain in the shadows and haunt us with a sense of unnamed loss. By facing our grief, however, we can embark on what Francis Weller has called 'an apprenticeship with sorrow':[12] the slow recognition and embrace of what we have lost to encounter the transformative potential of grief.

We turn, then, to ask the question, 'What is it we have forgotten?' We begin with soul grief.

The disenchantment of the world

'I don't believe in God, but I miss Him,' wrote Julian Barnes.[13] He captures something of the dilemma that many in the West feel in the twenty-first century: those who no longer find traditional religious beliefs plausible, yet feel keenly the loss of the communal and sacred world they represented. This loss has many faces, including the cultural loss of such things as buildings and architecture; the loss of community life that once orbited around shared customs; and the loss of symbolic meaning that a sacred perspective once took for granted.

To illustrate this loss, I am going to use an example that will be familiar to many readers: the symbol of the empty church. I bring this from my own (Scottish) context; for readers situated in other parts of the world and connected to different spiritual traditions, I hope that this will still speak to you. Often, the particular illuminates the universal. However, if my experience of soul grief is not yours, bear with me. I hope we will reach common ground.

There is poetry in an empty church. You don't have to be a believer to feel the pathos of a church building, locked and boarded, with grass in its gutters, its worn steps mute. A church building is far more than an institutional asset. It stands for something: a totem of common life; a witness of shared community; a porthole of solemn transitions; a place to approach our ancestors; and, perhaps above all, a site of the sacred.

It is true that some of our empty churches have come about because the burgeoning sects of nineteenth-century Britain sought to out-compete one another in capacity and so basically over-provided. Yet the pace of closure today signals a dramatic cultural shift; it is one that mirrors the decline in other forms of association, including political parties, voluntary associations and even the local pub.

Nearly thirty years ago, the Church of Scotland predicted that, at contemporary rates of decline, it would vanish altogether by the year 2033.[14] Graphs depicting social change rarely show straight lines, as predicted. Yet the scale of restructuring now under way in Scotland's national Church is startling, as congregations are amalgamated, churches closed and buildings sold off. At the time of writing,[15] the Church of Scotland has 25 church buildings up for sale, with a further 25 listed as 'under offer'.

Each one represents the death of a local community. At some point in the past, a group of people cared enough for their common life and faith to raise the funds to build a sacred space, where both the sacredness of human community and the mystery of God could be encountered. Stone and wood bore witness to the birth of this new life.

At Dalarossie, near Tomatin in the Scottish Highlands, stands an exquisite eighteenth-century Highland church, dedicated to the Celtic saint Fergus. It is built on the site of an older church and so dates back to the eighth century. Across its 1,300-year history, it has borne witness to the life of the local community, in mourning and celebration. The spinning seasons have mirrored its moods, kissing the land with ice, blossom, heat and harvest. A medieval font, unearthed from neighbouring glebe land, has been the focal point for welcoming generations of newborn children to the community. An upright stone slab with a circular hole – known as the 'bargain stone' – is believed to have witnessed the 'handfasting' of many marriages and the conclusion of land transactions, contracted by a handclasp through the hole. Around the church, stand ranks of gravestones, each of which marks the spot where a black knot of mourners gathered to bid farewell to one of their own. The church is a sermon in stone, telling the story of a local community – birth, marriage, business, death – reaching deep into a past when written records were few.

And now, as I write, it is up for sale. I stumbled upon it on a property website, where it says, 'Offers over £18,000.' I find this bald statement of its 'worth' shocking, as if the thirteen-hundred-year-old witness to the life of a living community could now be commodified and sold off at the price of a used Land Rover. Yet this story is being repeated across the country. Each church building is not only a warehouse or bijou residence in waiting, it is also the embodiment of the faith and hope, love and grief of an entire community.

In an interview for *The Herald*, the Very Revd Dr Susan Brown observed that, particularly in rural places, closing a church usually means closing the heart of the community.[16] The loss of such places invokes more than mere nostalgia: it represents the hollowing out of communities that have worshipped and worked together, in one place, for millennia. Perhaps the reason we do not feel this grief more keenly is that, in the West at least, we have been socialized into seeing ourselves as individuals and sovereign consumers. The church, we think, is for those who like that sort of thing; it is the club for those who share the same beliefs. We forget that, in many cases, it was the local community who raised the funds for their church building in the first place and, symbolically at least, it belongs to them.

But the empty church stands for a wider loss, too – the eclipse of the *sacred-in-community* – the sense that we have lost many of the sites where something mysterious and holy emerges in the spaces between neighbours sharing life together: something that is greater than the sum of its parts. In the past, it might have been experienced in such moments as women singing a waulking-song, as they gathered to thresh newly woven tweed, or by agricultural labourers sharing the rhythmic movements of harvest. It is well expressed in the South African notion of *ubuntu*, which roughly means 'I am because we are'. My identity is only complete in relationship with others. It is only with others that I can be most truly myself.

Dalarossie Church (and hundreds like it) illustrates the logic of late capitalism: the tearing of local community from the soil in which it flourished for millennia; and the transformation of its members from inclusive contributors to sovereign consumers – anonymous individuals whose lives revolve around the fulfilment of personal needs through the act of purchase. A question hangs over this shift. 'What if our primary human need is not to attend meticulously to our individual needs,' asks Steffi Bednarek, 'but rather to live our flawed and imperfect human lives in a participatory way, in continual relationship with all that lies outside of ourselves?'[17]

In the face of modernity, soul grief may not be consciously acknowledged, but it is expressed in our attempts to recreate what the German sociologist Ferdinand Tönnies called *Gemeinschaft*, which means community based on personal interactions. This is distinct from *Gesellschaft*, which means society consisting of impersonal relationships and formal roles. Debates about the relative merits of these forms of social interaction are not new but have been around since the nineteenth century. What has changed more recently is the attempt to assuage our soul grief by reconnecting to face-to-face activities and forging links to historic traditions. We can see this in such disparate examples as parkrun, historical re-enactment and the resurgence of interest in board games. Whether these compensate for the loss of our traditions is debatable. While pockets of community life remain, Weller notes, 'Modern technological society has forgotten what it feels like to be embedded in a living culture, one rich with stories and traditions, rituals and patterns of instruction that help us to become true human beings.'[18] In their absence, Danièle Hervieu-Léger has suggested that we have invented chains of memory that purport to reach back deep in time, including the reconstruction of 'Celtic' Christianity in the twentieth century and of pagan traditions from the 1940s onwards. These point to a hunger for a sacred connection that embraces the rhythms and seasons of the other-than-human world and that lives in respectful harmony with all life.

We turn then to consider the second of the ways in which we have forgotten something of what it means to be human: nature grief and our relationship to the other-than-human world.

The de-naturing of humanity

'Anyone who lives in a city will know the feeling of having been there too long,' writes Robert Macfarlane. 'The gorge-vision that streets imprint on us, the sense of blockage, the longing for surfaces other than glass, brick, concrete and tarmac.'[19] It is not that cities are bad: they too can be sites of the sacred and arenas of human flourishing. At its best, the earthly city can be a vision of the City of God, carved in stone. But what cities do is *insulate*.

Many of us carry a visceral need to immerse ourselves in

wild places. We would rather be on a mountainside in the teeth of a gale than trapped in the fug of a padded cinema seat on a dull Saturday afternoon. The sting of rain, the tendrils of icy water, the body check of the wind: these are what make our souls feel truly alive.

And yet we forget. We forget we are made of this stuff. We forget we emerged from nature and to nature we will return. Our limbed prototypes dragged themselves from the swamp, aeons ago, and evolved into a species that will one day return to join the carbon it has so recently released on the face of the earth. We forget that we are embodied beings, entirely dependent on an ecosystem for our survival. We behave as if we are somehow above nature, manipulating it from somewhere else.

I frequently hear the phrase 'getting out in nature', as if the natural world were always somewhere else: somewhere other than the valves of my beating heart. As Thomas Hübl has said, 'We don't live *on the planet*, but *as the planet*.'[20] Nearly fifty years ago, the poet-farmer Wendell Berry noticed our othering of nature. He commented:

> Once we see our place, our part of the world, as *surrounding* us, we have already made a profound division between it and ourselves. We have given up the understanding ... that our land passes in and out of our bodies just as our bodies pass in and out of our land ... so all who are living as neighbors here, human and plant and animal, are part of one another, and so cannot possibly flourish alone.[21]

We forget that, if we do manipulate nature, we do it from within. There *is* no 'somewhere else'. This point came home to me one day, when I announced that I was going to throw away an old suitcase. 'You can't throw it away,' a friend replied. 'There is no such place.'

Nature grief is not merely grief for something happening 'out there', as if we were dabbing our eyes at the sad spectacle of pollution, extinction and climate change from the safety of the dress circle. Nature grief is firstly about the grief we feel at the loss of our selves – our disconnection from body and soul, our visceral and unconscious selves – as well as from the other-than-human world on which we depend. Indeed, it is arguably this split within us that has enabled us to exploit and degrade the other-than-human world, sawing off the branch on which we are seated.

Forgetting we are earthen vessels, we have reimagined the human body as a fixable machine. We have construed human community as 'civilization', transcending the barbarism of the natural world. We have *de-natured* humanity; we have lost our essential characteristics and created the illusion that we can safely insulate ourselves from nature, at the same time as exploiting it. We no longer invest our own sweat in turning the soil. Our food comes to us from the far side of the globe, shrink-wrapped, on a plastic tray – an apt metaphor for our relationship with the other-than-human world.

The world we have recently created does not operate at a human scale. Some mornings, I am woken by the sound of an intense roar. In the fog of sleep, I sometimes wonder if I am hearing the Asiatic lion who lives a mile from me, at Edinburgh Zoo. But most often the tone is wrong: it lacks the deep, spine-tingling frequencies of this rare animal. I realize I am hearing the reverse thrust of jet engines at Edinburgh Airport, five miles away. When standing by a runway or motorway, we can quickly feel overwhelmed by the noise and power of the world we have created and sense our divorce from the organic world.

Cars and planes are part of the normal repertoire of today's transport system. It may seem odd to point to them to illustrate how human life has become skewed out of proportion with our environment. Yet it is precisely those things we take for granted that we need to question if we are to remember what we have lost. Each generation marvels at its own inventions; the next regards them as commonplace. Marcel Proust, who lived through the golden age of steam, famously declared that 'steamships insult the dignity of distance'. I wonder how much more he would he have thought the dignity of humanity might be insulted by what was to come.

We have created dystopian routines that are alien to the human organism. The indignities of the airport are the price we pay for speed. While being corralled into snaking queues, we are treated as suspected terrorists one minute and gullible consumers the next. No sooner have we replaced our boots and belts, after going through security, than we are steered on a compulsory path through bright lights and overpowering smells, and the lure of duty-free perfume and alcohol. Perhaps we sense that something is askew, but we can't say quite what. The glitz of an airport lounge is not designed to encourage us to reflect critically on the human journey from soil to asphalt. These radical and recent changes in the pace of human travel might not matter were it not for the fact that the transport sector is responsible for about a quarter of greenhouse gas emissions globally.

It is hard to keep in view such startling technological changes, yet the elderly in our society hold them in living memory. In the 1930s, my father grew up in a coastal village in Sutherland, where coal was unloaded from a steam puffer directly onto the beach. The only other power available came from peat, kerosene or the hotel's diesel generator. Barefoot schoolboys, chattering in Gaelic, learned to write English with chalk on slate. Today, his tablet is made from glass, not stone, and its learning apps are powered by artificial intelligence. That all this has happened in a single human lifetime is breathtaking. I wonder if we are still in shock, still to come to terms with our self-imposed exile from sand and soil, peat and rock?

The de-naturing of nature

As well as the grief of our isolation from the other-than-human world, we are now facing its disappearance. The litany of loss barely needs repeating: the ongoing pollution of our soil and air; the loss of biodiversity as we live through the sixth mass extinction; and the disruption from global warming. 'Whether or not we consciously recognise it,' Francis Weller says, 'the daily diminishment of species, habitats, and cultures is noted in our psyches.'[22] The psychoanalyst Wendy Greenspun has observed: 'People with climate distress and grief have begun to arrive on our clinical doorsteps.'[23]

Our grief is catalysed by our feelings of helplessness. At an individual level, we may wonder what difference our lifestyle choices can really make, when global climate summits are cynically infiltrated by vested interests from the fossil-fuel industries. At a societal level, we may feel still more paralysed, realizing that the dire warnings of climate scientists are not enough to jolt us all into necessary action. To rehash a metaphor, while scientists and environmentalists have gathered at the bow of the *Titanic* to scream for action, many passengers and crew down below are fretting about the economic harm of diverting the ship's course. It has been wryly observed that human beings are the only species that will become extinct because the alternatives were not economically viable.

Humanity is caught in a bind in which vested interests continue to pursue short-term personal gain that increases climate and ecological breakdown, while national governments seem impotent to meet basic climate goals. Already, the hope to 'keep 1.5 °C alive',[24] proclaimed at COP26, has been dashed. However, it is not just the oil lobby that is complicit. Many in western societies have bought in to a 'socially constructed silence' on the climate, where we tacitly agree not to draw attention to the emergency. This may be down to our own feelings of guilt at the contradiction between our values and our lifestyles, or a desire not to appear judgemental of others. Or it may simply be that the whole topic is overwhelming. Climate grief is often disenfranchised grief: a grief we feel but can't easily express.

Why do we forget?

We have seen how processes of industrialization and urbanization, and the whole juggernaut of modernity, have contributed to our amnesia towards soil and soul, and to the grief we feel at our forgetting. Before we turn to consider whether there can be anything redemptive in our grief, it is worth considering why we might forget in the first place. Forgetting, paradoxically, is often a symptom of something that is calling for attention. Analysing our forgetting may give us clues about what we need to remember: deeper parts of the self and community.

Freud thought that 'there is a type of forgetting that is motivated by repression'.[25] Repression is a psychological defence in which painful aspects of the self, or traumatic memories, are split off from conscious awareness and pushed out of sight into the unconscious. Often, these are not accessible to memory at all; or if they are, they are experienced as 'disavowed' or belonging somewhere else.

Modernity, and the rift that the industrial-urban world drove between humans and the environment, has been called the 'original trauma'[26] in the story of our forgetting. This trauma has been compounded by the industrialization of war in the twentieth century, which enabled the mass killings occasioned by the First World War, the Holocaust and the atomic bomb.

As a protective measure, overwhelming traumatic experiences are typically split off from consciousness, leaving another part of the brain still able to function. When these experiences remain unprocessed and inaccessible, post-traumatic stress can become chronic. Something similar may happen at a societal level: unable to cope with the violence we are doing to our environment and to one another, we repress our memory of the unprecedented changes we have lived through. We feel our disconnection from soil and soul only in the legacy of chronic symptoms. Steffi Bednarek applies this logic to the climate emergency to explain why we are unable to heed the warnings of scientists in the face of its existential threat. 'Chronic trauma cannot be resolved with logic, pressure, demands, advice or pleas. It is therefore highly unlikely that climate information and statistics can mobilize the frozen or irrational parts of society.'[27] This helps explain our forgetting of our own biological nature and how it can be that 'the degradation of life is ongoing in a world that faces mass extinctions while keeping the machinery of capitalism going at full speed'.[28]

The spirituality of collective grief

What are we to make of our collective griefs, our shared well of pain? How can we begin to heal the trauma of the modern world? What invitation to renewed connection, insight and personal growth might we hear as we acknowledge our grief for soil and soul?

Many of those working in the field of collective trauma acknowledge that we can't easily process this individually: 'Collective trauma needs a collective container for collective healing.'[29] Yet we have lost many of the traditions, rituals and support structures that once enabled us to process our grief. In Ancient Israel, for example, the Book of Psalms provided a particular genre of poetry – the psalm of lament – that enabled the community to gather and voice its woes to God. Today, our climate anxiety or the grief of our existential loneliness cannot easily be assuaged by a one-to-one encounter in the therapy room. My grief is not mine alone, but ours; I need to connect with others to find healing.

In the absence of traditional containers, and in the face of our 'socially constructed silence' about the climate emergency, several community-based models have emerged to give a voice to grief.[30] Just as Death Cafes have emerged globally to destigmatize talking about death, Climate Cafes have adapted this model to help to nurture open conversations in which anxieties about the climate and ecological crises can be expressed. They help to normalize participants' feelings and emphasize their collective response.

Other approaches look to the wisdom of indigenous cultures to provide clues to the kind of collective grief rituals that might enable us to heal. The psychotherapist Francis Weller, who has been leading grief rituals for decades, sees his work as an attempt to recover the *commons of the soul* – the stories, traditions, rituals and patterns of instruction bequeathed by a living culture – that sustained and nourished both individual and community for tens of thousands of years.[31] While nature grief and soul grief are based on our forgetting of our true selves, such grief work helps us to remember what we have lost and to work through our collective grief within the safe container of shared rituals.

Historic faith traditions also offer resources for collective healing. The Abrahamic faiths have often been criticized for advancing an anthropocentric view of humanity, which places human beings beyond nature and justifies the exploitation of the other-than-human world. While such theologies have undoubtedly existed, they are not the only way of reading these traditions. Indeed, within Christian theology, for example, we can point to the resources of liberation theology or the Franciscan and Celtic traditions to find a very different relationship imagined between humans and the other-than-human. In the 30 years between the first and second edition of Ian Bradley's *God is Green*, for example, a rich vein of theological reflection on the environment has emerged, which he reviews in a new introduction.[32] This thinking should not be overlooked as we seek resources to recover the cultural memory of all we have lost.

Soil and soul

I began this chapter by saying that our forgetting of our human relationship with soil and soul is not two forms of amnesia, but one. As Wendell Berry has put it:

the 'environmental crisis' is no such thing; it is not a crisis of our environs or surroundings; it is a crisis of our lives as individuals, as family members, as community members, and as citizens. We have an 'environmental crisis' because we have consented to an economy in which by eating, drinking, working, resting, traveling and enjoying ourselves, we are destroying the natural, the God-given, world.[33]

The environmental crisis is, at root, a crisis of the soul. I hope it is clearer now that we cannot heal one without the other. Neither the cleverest instruments of technology nor unfettered market forces will be able to provide the solution that will restore humanity to a sustainable, respectful, life-preserving relationship with the other-than-human world. We need to *remember our roots in soil and soul*, and return to a values-based and wisdom-based approach to the other-than-human world. We need to rediscover a human 'soulfulness' or interiority that allows us to recognize our own grief – one that helps us to work through the trauma and dissociation that prevents us from facing the climate and ecological crisis squarely. This will involve giving voice to our collective grief over our exiled condition and accepting our cultural ills as symptoms of losing touch with life lived in human and sacred community.

All is not loss

Owning our collective grief will be painful, but perhaps it is a part of the 'necessary suffering' we must endure to grow beyond it. Throughout this book, I have explored grief's invitation to an enlarged world, where we may find ourselves with new insight, a bigger heart, and deeper relationships with one another and with the other-than-human world – both nature and the transcendent.

With grief there are no guarantees. Some losses are just painful, with no redemptive arc. We cope with them as best we can. Where grief seems hopeless, perhaps the most we can hope for is to work through our grief until the pain lessens and we learn to carry what we have loved and lost within.

But the hope of grief explored here, witnessed in the example of many who have mourned, is that grief does not always have the final word. We can find in grief a spiritual call, a quiet invitation to inner transformation and the growth of the soul. Although loss, in its many strands, is woven into the human story, there is a larger pattern in the warp and weft. Yes, grief is everywhere: it is the common experience of being human. And yet, as I have suggested throughout this book, grief may visit us with unexpected gifts, whispering as it comes: *all is not loss*.

Notes

1 B. McKibben, 2021, *An Idea Can Go Extinct*, London: Penguin, pp. 62–3.
2 F. Weller, 2015, *The Wild Edge of Sorrow: Rituals of renewal and the sacred work of grief*, Berkeley, CA: North Atlantic Books, p. xvi.
3 C. S. Lewis, 1977, *Mere Christianity*, Glasgow: Fount, p. 136.
4 Alastair McIntosh, 2004, *Soil and Soul: People versus corporate power*, London: Aurum, p. 1.
5 O. Chadwick, 1974, *The Secularization of the European Mind in the Nineteenth Century*, Cambridge: Cambridge University Press, p. 100.
6 Quoted in Danièle Hervieu-Léger, 2000, *Religion as a Chain of Memory*, Cambridge: Polity, p. 13.
7 See D. MacLaren, 2004, *Mission Implausible: Restoring credibility to the church*, Bletchley: Paternoster Press, chs 2 and 3.
8 A. Giddens, 1990, *The Consequences of Modernity*, Cambridge: Polity, p. 21.
9 I survey some of the other ideological elements of the Enlightenment in *Mission Implausible*, ch. 2.
10 H. II. Bryson, 2024, 'Decolonizing Psychotherapy', in S. Bednarek (ed.), *Climate, Psychology, and Change: Reimagining psychotherapy in an era of global disruption and climate anxiety*, Berkeley, CA: North Atlantic Books, pp. 91–105, p. 99.
11 S. Bednarek, 2024, 'Climate Change, Fragmentation, and Collective Trauma', in Bednarek (ed.), *Climate, Psychology, and Change*, pp. 145–58, p. 152.
12 Weller, *Wild Edge*, p. xxii.

13 J. Barnes, 2008, *Nothing to be Frightened of*, London: Jonathan Cape, p. 1.

14 Cited in C. G. Brown, 2001, *The Death of Christian Britain*, London: Routledge, p. 5.

15 December 2024.

16 M. Smith, 2023, 'Is There Still Time to Save the Church of Scotland?', *The Herald*, at https://www.heraldscotland.com/politics/viewpoint/23537181.mark-smith-still-time-save-church-scotland, accessed 14.04.2025.

17 Bednarek, Introduction, in Bednarek (ed.), *Climate, Psychology, and Change*, pp. 1–8, p. 5.

18 Weller, *Wild Edge*, p. xx.

19 Robert Macfarlane, 2017, *The Wild Places*, London: Granta Books, pp. 6–7.

20 T. Hübl, 2024, Foreword, in Bednarek (ed.), *Climate, Psychology, and Change*, pp. xv–xviii, p. xv.

21 W. Berry, 1977, *The Unsettling of America: Culture & Agriculture*, San Francisco: Sierra Club Books, p. 22.

22 Weller, *Wild Edge*, p. 46.

23 W. Greenspun, 2024, 'Frozen in Trauma on a Warming Planet', in Bednarek (ed.), *Climate, Psychology, and Change*, pp. 65–76, p. 66.

24 A slogan popularized at the COP26 climate summit, calling on countries to limit global warming to within 1.5°C above pre-industrial levels.

25 S. Freud, 1975, *The Psychopathology of Everyday Life*, trans. A. Tyson, Harmondsworth: Pelican, p. 44.

26 C. Glendinning, 1994, *'My Name Is Chellis, and I'm in Recovery from Western Civilization'*, Boulder, CO: Shambhala, p. 57.

27 Bednarek, 'Climate Change, Fragmentation', p. 154.

28 Bednarek, 'Climate Change, Fragmentation', p. 152.

29 Bednarek, 'Climate Change, Fragmentation', p. 155.

30 For example, initiatives such as The Work That Reconnects Network, Living With the Climate Crisis, and Active Hope, cited in T. Macagnino, 2024, 'Why Aren't We Talking about Climate Change?', in Bednarek (ed.), *Climate, Psychology, and Change*, pp. 49–63, p. 62.

31 Weller, *Wild Edge*, p. xx.

32 I. Bradley, 2020, *God Is Green*, London: Darton, Longman and Todd, pp. 6f.

33 W. Berry, 2021, *What I Stand For Is What I Stand On*, London: Penguin, pp. 58–9.

Acknowledgement of Sources

The author and publisher acknowledge with thanks permission to use extracts under copyright:

C. Day-Lewis, 1962, 'Walking Away', in *The Gate*, Jonathan Cape. Used by permission of Peters Fraser & Dunlop (www.petersfraserdunlop.com) on behalf of the Estate of C. Day-Lewis.

Norman MacCaig, 2011, 'So Many Summers', in *The Poems of Norman MacCaig*, Edinburgh: Polygon, p. 216. Reproduced with permission of the Licensor through PLSclear.

Index of Names and Subjects

ageing 20, 22, 26, 28, 34, 36–7, 40, 43–6, 50
aloneness xix, 2, 10, 34, 38, 59–61, 63, 97, 99, 100, 120–1, 140
anxiety 2, 6–7, 10, 12, 21–2, 27–8, 54, 78, 90, 93, 106, 113, 114, 130, 140
assisted dying 40
autonomy xv, 34, 39–40, 50, 117

Bednarek, Steffi 129, 133, 139
Benedict, St. 23, 73
bereavement ix, xiv, xxvi, 1–16, 27, 60, 97–8, 99, 100, 103–4, 107, 109, 110, 116
Boas, Simon 26, 30, 31, 49
Boulding, Maria 88, 95
Bowlby, John 8, 9, 10
Bradley, Ian ix, 30, 72, 141
Buddhism 25, 26, 31

Cain, Susan 56–7
Calidas, Tamsin 70, 100
Cave, Nick 3, 4, 7, 11, 13, 15, 28, 124
Church of Scotland 131
Christianity xx, 31, 38, 43, 94, 134, 141
climate 129, 130, 135, 138–40, 142
crofting 69

Day-Lewis, Cecil 54–5
death ix, xiv, xv, vii, 1–2, 3, 5–7, 11, 12, 14–15, 19–32, 34, 37, 39, 40, 44, 45, 48, 49–50, 56, 58, 61, 72, 95, 99, 100, 102–4, 116, 120, 121, 124, 131, 132, 140
dependence xv, 34–50
Didion, Joan 2, 3, 12, 124
disability xv, 34, 35, 36, 40, 43, 50
Dundas, Henry 81–3, 87
dying ix, xv, 13, 14, 23, 25, 27–30, 34, 39–40, 46, 48–50, 115, 116, 121, 125

empathy 11, 14, 72, 98, 102, 103
employment law 103
environment 4, 12, 63, 67, 125, 130, 136, 139, 141, 142
Erikson, Erik 45, 62
extinction xiii, 127, 135, 138, 140

failure xvi, 81–95, 109, 115, 116
false self 93, 108–9
forgetting xvi, 3, 9, 11, 21, 106, 127–43
freedom 5, 47, 56, 61, 113
Freud, Sigmund 7, 12, 20, 21, 26, 139

INDEX OF NAMES AND SUBJECTS

God xxi, xxv, 12, 13, 35, 36, 42–3, 45, 63, 77, 88, 92, 93, 95, 130, 132, 140, 142
grief
  anticipatory 104
  collective xvi, 127–43
  disenfranchised xvi, 97–111, 138
  impact of xxvi, 1, 2, 3, 5, 8
  invitation of xv, 4, 6, 7, 9, 13, 23, 26, 45, 46, 50, 57, 58, 59, 61, 62, 63, 74, 86, 89, 90, 92, 93, 94, 95, 107, 109, 121, 140, 143
  private 99–101
  models of 10
  spirituality of xvii, xix, xxiii, xxv, 4, 6, 8, 10–15, 29, 41, 43–4, 46, 48, 58, 86, 90, 104, 106, 115, 140–3
guilt ix, x, 2, 6, 7–8, 93, 104, 106–7, 109, 116, 138

Highland Clearances 68, 69, 70, 79n1
Holloway, Richard 70
Hopkins, Gerard Manley 76, 96n17

illness xv, xxiv, 4, 28, 29, 34, 35, 38–9, 40, 46, 48, 50, 99, 103, 121, 125
impermanence 24, 26
industrialization 128, 129, 139
IVF 100

Jesus 38, 42, 43, 63, 94, 95
Job, Book of 16, 92
Jung, Carl 25, 43–5, 108, 120

Kavanagh, Jennifer 90
Kellehear, Alan 48

Lewis, Clive S. 8, 11, 20, 77, 80n19, 127
loneliness xiv, 6, 8, 27, 40, 63, 87, 89, 101, 102, 104, 121, 130, 140
loss
  ambiguous 103–4
  necessary xv, 55, 56, 58, 59, 122–3, 142
  pervasive xiv, xvi, xvii, xix, 86

MacCaig, Norman 65, 78
meaning 7, 12, 44, 45, 49, 73, 110, 111, 130, 131
memento mori 23–5, 27, 30
Montaigne, Michel de 20, 23, 29, 30, 31, 37
Moran, Joe 45, 81, 85, 86, 87, 91, 94, 113
mortality xv, 13, 19–32, 37, 61, 62, 120, 121
mourning xvi, 9, 10, 12, 97, 99, 103, 132

nature xvi, 12, 29, 31, 129, 130, 134–7, 141, 142
nostalgia xv, 65–79, 132

Orkney xix, 29, 47

Parkes, Colin M. 4, 8, 10, 15
parting ix, xv, 53–64

regret xvi, 22, 27, 34, 109, 113–25
religion ix, x, xx, xxi, xxii, xxv, 12, 23, 45, 56, 71, 94, 109, 111, 116, 130
ritual 15, 109–11, 116, 130, 134, 140, 141
Rohr, Richard 44, 62, 108

secularization 128, 129

self 5, 6, 7, 9, 44, 59, 60, 62, 74, 93, 104, 108, 115, 122, 136, 139
Self, Will 121
sex 22
sexuality 97, 98
shame xvi, 2, 22, 75, 76, 81, 84, 87, 88, 95, 97–111, 115, 120
soil xvi, 125, 127–9, 133, 136, 137, 139, 140, 142
soul xvi, xx, 45, 49, 50, 67, 120, 125, 127–34, 136, 139, 140, 141, 143
spirituality ix, x, xiii–xxvi, 4, 9, 12, 13, 15, 21, 25, 37, 40, 41, 43, 45, 48, 49, 50, 57, 58, 72–9, 85, 86, 93, 95, 104, 106, 107, 109, 116, 121, 122, 127, 131, 140, 143
stillbirth 100, 101, 103, 110
success 44, 81–95
suffering ix, xvii, 13, 26, 34, 38, 46, 48, 50, 92, 100, 116, 121, 127, 142

suicide 4, 11, 14, 88, 99

therapy xiv, 15, 60, 106, 138, 140
transcendence xxiv, 4, 12, 13, 15, 45, 77, 78, 104, 142

urbanization 128, 139

Viorst, Judith xxviii, 56

Weller, Francis xxvi, 4, 15, 93, 111, 116, 127, 130, 134, 138, 141
Wertheimer, Alison 4, 11, 14
Whorton, Bob 26, 38, 49
Winnicott, Donald 59
Worden, William J. 10

Yalom, Irvin 3, 5, 12, 20, 22, 25, 26, 32, 36, 49, 60, 102

www.ingramcontent.com/pod-product-compliance
Lightning Source LLC
Chambersburg PA
CBHW060607080526
44585CB00013B/717